I AM A
STRANGE
LOOP

I AM A STRANGE LOOP

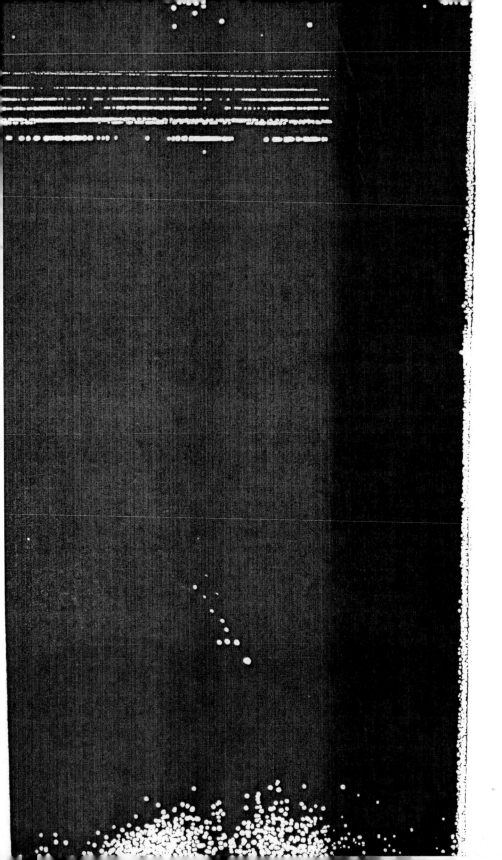

TAMA
RANGI
LOOP

I AM A
FRANGI
POOP

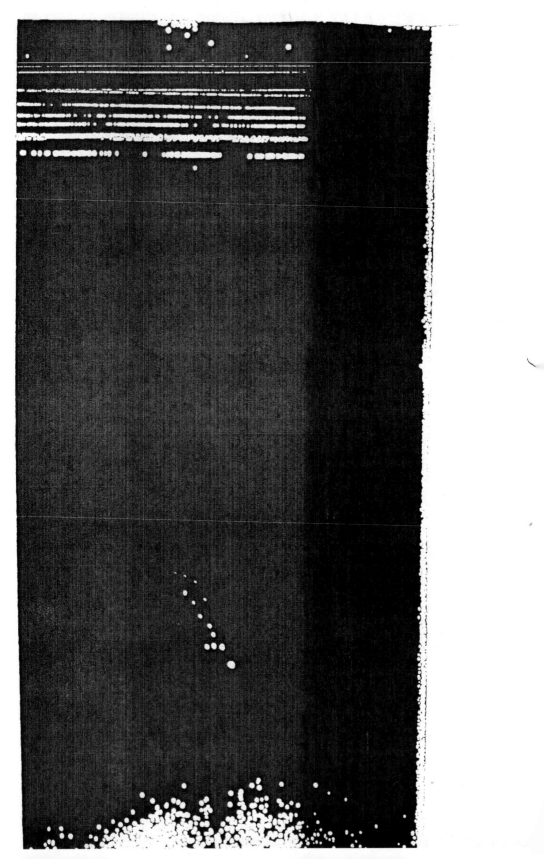

ANNA
RANGI
LOOP

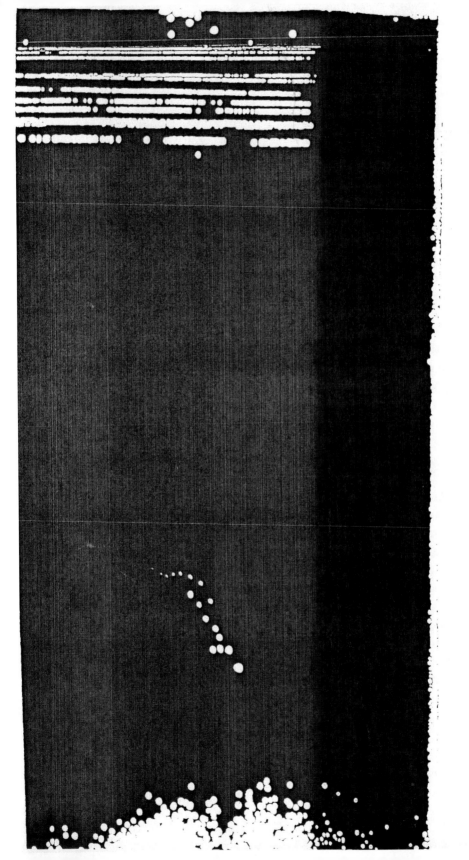

THE OCCULATIOMORBIT
https://endythekid.blogspot.com/
https://kanshiketsu.bandcamp.com/
https://www.lulu.com/spotlight/lunde

REISSUE

ISBN: 978-1-312-10458-7

©2023 Eric Lunde

I AM A COPY OF A COPY OF A STRANGE LOOP

ERIC LUNDE

TABLE OF CONTENTS:

Preface..............................21
LIVING IN SHORTHAND (or "On the Stenographic Life") ….....…….29
I am a copy of a copy of a copy of a strange loop………………..46
Here come the strange loops… or not…………………….92

Preface

What makes the employment of technology as either metaphor, allegory, or analogy problematic is the elliptical nature of the argument (is the conclusion drawn from nature or from artifice? Which came first? The technology? Or is the conduct drawn from the technology?) The argument certainly seems unreliable from one perspective: if the conclusion drawn is not from nature, then how do we know the conclusion is authentic? Does one deliberately seek these analogies out? Or do they present themselves?

That designation of authenticity is not necessarily applicable, nor should any argument be gauged according to such criteria. The mechanisms suggested by various technologies seem illustrative of many processes inherent in human cognition and behavior; suggestions that can further assist anyone's comprehension of processes, including the mechanism of comprehension itself.

That anyone should avert their attention from the theories suggested by technological processes simple because they are "inauthentic" would be a grave disservice to our continual progress.

Many philosophers and theorists have responded to various mechanisms as not manifestations of their theories but illustrative of them, demonstrative. Case in point is Douglas Hofstadter's "I Am A Strange Loop." In it, Mr. Hofstadter employees various descriptions of technological processes to illustrate and elucidate his points about consciousness and cognition, particularly video feedback and copying machines.

I read Mr. Hofstadter's account with great interest, despite the periodic creative flourishes (no disrespect intended here, but I do believe Mr. Hofstadter admitted as much). The employment of technological processes to demonstrate philosophical premises does not at all impede their significance, and I think "I Am A Strange Loop" accomplishes this remarkably well.

But the fact of the matter is that, given my own experience with technology, my own practice and procedures, explorations and experiments, something was lacking or overlooked that could impact the theories he was elucidating. And it is not my intention to counter Mr. Hofstadter's arguments but to augment them by illustrating the other processes Mr. Hofstadter overlooked.

The procedures of audio and video technology that gives rise to feedback certainly illustrate the self-constructing nature of endless loops, the infinite recursion at the heart of matter and mind, mathematics and consciousness. Reproduction of the same increases exponentially into a state in which the difference is split amongst the multiplications of the same: the same no longer appears so and becomes something else.

But this is only in regards to the same, or, rather, the inherent differentiations within recursions of the same. And in regards to the construction of the self, of consciousness and cognition, feedback is a vital and essential mechanism.

Such reproductive, duplicative technologies also suggest the modes by which we appropriate information. The processes of recording and photocopying do not so much as represent but reproduce, duplicate, copy. That no information is entirely pure when so reproduced may not be problematic in the generalizations required when we interpret conduct and/or practice according to criteria derived from the analogy with technology, which is the inherent danger of doing so.

This is not saying that the conclusions drawn by Mr. Hofstadter are wrong; they are simply incomplete. And it is, then, an opportunity for someone else to explore the gaps, opening up yet other opportunities and possibilities for further comprehension of our activities and the functions that make these activities possible.

Now, admittedly I am not the best authority on the matters of human cognition and social interaction. I possess nothing in terms of pedigree or profession, I am something of a "lay" theorists whose own curiosities regarding these aspects of human nature have lead me to this.

So, if I could sit down with Mr. Hofstadter I would say, yes, inherent feedback processes of audio/video media are, indeed, illustrative of self-organization and infinite recursion, and, therefore, somewhat analogous with human consciousness and self-construction, but the other aspect here, the part I have personally explored, which is certainly not the intended manner, is that of reduplication, i.e.: copying the copy itself (see endnote).

Having read the book, I began reflecting on my own experiences with these techniques and what they might suggest as an extension of Mr. Hofstadter's research. If technology, by analogy, suggests certain patterns and processes of cognition and social interaction, then, it would be "natural" that the type of process I have been engaged in would suggest further elaborations.

Pardon then my own indulgence. The processes of reduplication are not essentially the mode intended by the manufacturer, you might say. Photocopy machines, audio and video recorders (of the analogue sort) were intended to faithfully duplicate events, actions, and information. To faithfully, accurately reproduce is an impossibility because in no way could any technology ever actually and accurately reproduce anything, given the shortcomings of the technology, like focal length, discrepancies in materials, machine hum, etc.

As it is, in art one works with the characteristics of the medium to invite and elaborate a distinct project. One exploits the shortcomings for one's advantage. Even then, there are characteristics of, say, recording medium that are specific to them. A certain 'ambience' or texture the characteristics impose upon the content.

And the use of said medium in a way not intended by the originator of the medium (engineer and/or manufacturer), or of the accepted manner of use established by the social, is somewhat deviant. Mr. Hofstadter's video feedback loops are certainly deviant in this sense, a "happy accident" of the technology discovered through chance that leads to the various realizations he and others have discovered.

Reduplication is also one of those deviant uses that also points toward further realizations of how the world works, either as metaphor or analogy. A copy of a copy of a copy… ad infinitum, seems to suggest a complimentary theory regarding human cognition, development, and social interaction, particularly regarding ideas, the generation of ideas, and the development of ideas.

Despite the fact that we cannot accurately represent to others and ourselves ideas about the world or about the world itself, as well as about ourselves and others, we continue to assume accuracy or fidelity and, oddly enough, disparage those that fail to do so. Accuracy is equated with authenticity, an edict that has guided medieval and classical thought. We assume for the mechanics of mind and self that somehow we can obtain accuracy that our representations can be "clear", accurate, nearly verbatim.

That is, of course, not the case at all. We do not "mirror" the world in our minds, nor do we "photograph" the world, or simply copy it. The variables in the equipment form variables in the content, and content as well as form and appearance, is reduplicated in our minds. Unlike the eye, the ear cannot distinguish what we want to hear; we can concentrate, but we cannot filter signals and information. And because of this, we often confuse audio signals, resulting in imperfections in the mental duplicates we generate.

For example, when I was around 12, I tried to record favorite records using a portable cassette recorder, placing the microphone next to the speaker and recording the recording in ambient. This, because I had no access to line-in, direct recording, resulted in "unwanted', unintended audio content disturbing the recording, resulting in less than favorable, and less than faithful, results. To this day, when I hear one of the songs I recorded in this manner, quite often I cannot listen to it without such disturbances being recalled, as if part of the recording itself: either a sibling yelling, or the crash of a pan, or a mischievous comment made intentionally by my brother.

Thomas Metzinger[1] likened the self as something like a window, a transparency of consciousness that we both are and see through. And this is fine, almost perfect, even as it is a metaphor, but what we should not assume here is that the processing of information that this "window" both appropriates and generates does not occur without some variations, due to inherent flaws in the material (as old pane glass contains), processing flaws (due to shortcomings in the person's cognitive construct), processing advantages (due to the advanced or superior improvements in a person's cognitive construct) and in the nature of cognitive process itself. And it is my contention here that our cognitive process, in how things are processed and how the process itself develops, is reliant upon processes of duplication, reduplication, feedback and amplification. It is not merely a mechanism of reproduction, representation, and reflection: the mind is not a hall of mirrors where images of things bounce

---
[1] See Metzinger's *"Being No One"*, 2003 MIT Press

about with the ideas we have of them, nor do the minds reflect or represent them. Our minds, and, ultimately, the social patterns that disseminate and process these ideas, are indeed copying machines, but copy machines making copies of other copies. As you can see, the infinitely recursive loop that "I AM" is not merely the re-iteration of the self-same, but of copies and copies of copies thereof.

I hope in some way that my project here first communicates my ideas despite my lack of pedigree and ultimately contributes to, and compliments, the work currently being done regarding neuro-cognitive processes, the construct of the self and social mechanisms.

LIVING IN SHORTHAND (or "On the Stenographic Life")

Do we build a life? Or is one built for us? What is "a life"? We know what life is even as we must weigh factual, counterfactual, and contrary considerations, sure, but what is this thing we call " a life"? As opposed to the simple fact of existence, or animation, of being, "a life" is how we describe our being, the singular trajectory of our existence, by ourselves, the biographical details of our being and having been.

But be more specific here: *a* life? We seem to think so. We inherit the idea that we are of a single and inviolable entity, a life that we have built. We are proud inventors of our existence.

A long time ago, I invented for myself a curious axiom about time, specifically, my time: regard each moment as single and inviolable. It was a manner by which I fabricated a framing device in order to assume a certain degree of security. It was how I viewed the continuous pattern of life as it evolved.

Let us say this is true for the moment. Let us assume for a moment that the "I" does exist, this "I" which we have crafted. As it is in time, it would certainly be a single and inviolable instant, a cohesive pattern of continuity that supports the notion of a coherent whole.

As we might understand now, this is mere shorthand for a far more involved project, shorthand whose simplicity assists by lessening the complexity that is there and allows us the conceit of coherence. We come to rely on our "existential shorthand" to make things easier for us to process. The "I" is merely an ideogram that allows us to identify and refer, an anagram for the elements that compose the construct of the person employing the shorthand to describe him/her self and their relation to other selves.

This shorthand is a survival skill; it simplifies things to terms easily comprehended. It allows for easier negotiation through life without burdening ourselves with the more factual complexity that we choose to ignore.

If we do, indeed, build a life, how do we do it? Let us say for the sake of argument that we do build a life, fabricate a mechanism for living. Do we do it through subtraction? Through addition? Through the alteration between both? Or both simultaneously? What are our options?

Sculpture or collage? These are not the only options, but the argument suggests their suitability as allegory: do we build a life as sculpture, subtracting material till we arrive at the form we desire? Or do we remove material from other forms and re-arrange these portions in a form we surprise ourselves with?

All in all, I suppose I side with collage, the taking away from form A and repositioning it within form B. But even then, even through the shorthand of an allegory formed from an artistic medium, we have not yet built a life, nor do I even think it is possible to, especially as a single and inviolable entity.

But why "inviolability"? It is important to us to think of our lives as continuous, as a point A-to-point B linear progression. To think otherwise, we assume here, is to make ourselves vulnerable to some unforeseen assault. That of course is not the case at all, or wouldn't be if we weren't so mired into our convenience of the static idyll we enjoy.

Having place and identity (or purpose as provided by identity) is, of course, not the same as recognizing position and function. And it would, within the context of our day to day living, the social construct of our living, make sense to grasp, however tenuous it is, at any support that would ease our way through the given circumstances.

Don't assume that this is primarily an Occidental issue and that some exotic variant exists somewhere in Oriental thought that would "release us" from this quandary: given our current global consciousness, this assumption of inviolability and continuity, the assumption of linear and continuous progression is, as universal, emblematic of the human condition. And as such, we should not assume that the prevalence and unanimity of such a condition represents a truth. It only means that it is prevalent and ordinary.

So what we struggle with, or do not, given the shorthand for living that we employ, is the fact that we are not always available to ourselves, that through time we are barely the "I" we once were, that the instant that we declare ourselves as "I", while assuming it is inviolable and discrete in itself, it is gone. " 'I' is like the present tense marked by 'now'...." [2]

And then, again, it could be regarded as such, and why not? Nothing prevents us from saying it is so, and from our perspective, it appears to be. We assume a continuum of events as evidence of a solid, continuous

---

[2] pg. 112, *Counterfactuals*, David Lewis, 2008 Blackwell

whole, which is fine, but in actuality there is so much interference and noise in that continuum that we can only assume, and then act on and from, that there is such a thing.

What would it be like to grasp the now? Evasive, certainly for us: we rely on our sense of past and future to direct our activities, our negotiations and, more importantly, to establish the continuity of ourselves. We require past and future for coordinate points of reference.

Without them, would "I" disappear? I would speculate that, yes, it would, or, at least, it would not be the "I" we are accustomed to. Less the "continuum" of elements that, as an accordion, folds into this one index point we call "I", and more the compendium of discrete packets, a compendium that we would not recognize as the singular occurrence of multiple events, but the multiple occurrence of singular events.

What differentiates us from animals, it is thought, is their lack of self-consciousness. But what serves animals in the absence of self-consciousness? Here I would offer a speculation gathered not from evidence but from observation and thought experiments. I offer my cats, who don't seem to be involved in past/present thinking at all. It is speculated that memory only exists as a triggering mechanism; various contingencies determine action, but not conscious memory. Instinct being one of those triggering mechanisms directs action towards fulfillment.

But having no "memory" per se, as an envisioned revisitation of past events, I think my cats are subject to renewal, that every moment is a renewal of their being present: they only know of the now and have no notion of extension into time or even space. Everything operates on triggers, which must be on standby; they are not recalled nor evoked. They are perpetually at the ready, waiting for the right contingencies to present themselves and from these direct the actions of the animal.

In this sense, having a self is a liability. Lets be clear here; I'm not advocating that an animal sense is true or favorable, but I would say that there isn't, at the base, that much difference between us, that removing the extraneous modes of self and the maintenance of it, would "return" us to a more acute sense of Now then what we currently possess. And yes, even in having done so, in having evicted the self we could still function as humans, possibly better. But I digress.

Where do you end and the world begin? Ontological continuity is generally ascertained through the coordination of evidence, the having been there, memory, events…each serving as both increments in the linear progression of our lives and indices by which we catalogue and collate.

Ontological continuity is realized in temporal organization, not spatial: the spatial organization of ontological continuity is not realizable. Here, the continuum we assume is composed of discrete elements, existing in and out in time as both memory and consciousness serves and as experienced (which I might assume is what David Bohm might have meant by the implicate order of matter). The self is entirely grounded on the substrate of the temporal. The Self is a clock.

So, necessarily, we would have to determine if existence is continuous or composed, continuous in progression or composed of discrete packets of elements and events.

And this is where things get a little tricky, but why? Why should it be 'contradictory'? We should accept that there is simultaneity, that there is a continuum of discrete elements, a continuity of the discontinuous, an implicate order that communicates the explicate order, a folding and unfolding. We assume a continuity of self in that, as a temporally realized entity, we assemble from the increments a "whole" of a larger unity: from minutes we know hours, but barely register minutes in our experience. And like time, we know the self from the "selves" we barely register. The self-clock, registering in a vertical axis, is not distributed topologically along a horizontal axis. That is to say, the self is not a topologically constructed entity, there is no material evidence of its being, only as it is thought. Does this qualify it as an abstraction? No not entirely. If we assume a materiality of thought, then the parameters of the self are realized there in the materiality of thought, but are not evidence of the self. This sort of consistency is only available to us from the evidence of thought and, particularly, memory. And it is through memory that we form the predictable periodicity of the self: the return of self through memory. The persistence of the self could be likened to the persistent of vision that cinema and flipbooks rely upon to convey the illusion of motion. Single, discrete frames of still images strung together then run sequentially in rapid fashion would, by themselves, remain single frames of unrelated images. But only through the persistence of vision, the ability of the retina to retain an image for a short duration, only through this feature of vision is movement discerned.

And we can attribute the continuity of the self to a similar thing: the persistence of memory informs our assumption of continuity. The self, then, is a product of such persistence, and, again, it is achieved more through our inclination towards temporal extension made possible by our cognitive mechanism.

Through this persistence of a "felt" image of our selves, derived from memory, sense, locution, and location, we are lead to believe in a solidity that, although not actual, provides the necessary "proof" that we are here, have been here, and will be here.

The case for the self as an inviolable element, as some sort of operative encased or embedded in the brain, can be made but only as to how it is so felt and therefore believed; it is not known, nor confirmed, but believed. There is a certain faith in our belief in our self, that it will occur, it will return, which of course is maintained without regard to the fact that it is also a transitory and ephemeral by-product of cognition.

Would the self continue if the brain were excised from the body? The proverbial brain-in-the-box scenario usually concludes with the belief that the seat of the self is the brain. And that would be partially true, for at least the circuitry is there. But a brain-in-a-box, it would seem to me, is merely a brain-in-a-box. Is it aware? Possibly, but it cannot tell you this. Is it cognizant of itself? Probably not. Does it recall itself; does it have memory of itself? Possibly, but in that it lacks the proper "format", a body whose sense-array provides information to the brain, it cannot express nor articulate these memories. In some way, I would speculate, there would be a requirement of a "full body recall", even in the slightest memory. More than likely all self-awareness functions have ceased and, in that it is divorced from the body and the body's neural circuitry, there is nothing to refer to, no date, and no feedback. There is a requirement of a physiological dimension of the neurological circuitry the whole body provides; an extension by which the mind knows itself as Self. The self is only as it is "informed", compatible with the body. I mean, the brain is not sufficient in itself for the location of the self: it relies on the information and feedback provided by the body. If, say, we transplanted the brain-organ into another body, it is unlikely that the person would "wake up" to being that person in another body. No, if the brain responded at all, it would more than likely adapt to its "new environment" and become yet another person, probably "stuck" with the memories of the person of that brain, but not with the identity native to that brain. A+B would equal C, not A again nor B again. Once again, there is an illusion of equilibrium and continuity that is essential to survival. We have long assumed that we are trapped in the body, that self-consciousness equates with a specific and inviolable entity that can be segregated from the context of the body. Recent cognitive research certainly refutes the concept of the homunculus self, conducting and operating the body. But it is the body that conducts us, or, more probably, a simultaneous superimposition of parallel processes and procedures that inadvertently lend credence to the notion of continuity but only to conceal the multiplicity of events that actually occur at any given moment in the life of the entity. The self is an emergent epiphenomenon, emerging and evolving through corporal/neural feedback that amplifies and extends the notion of the self over the duration of a lifetime.

We cannot "know the now" because it would be detrimental to our cognitive process. Consciousness requires a referent, a point from which to coordinate the coordinates of the topography of life. Without this, the entity is either lost in the conjectures he/she has fashioned for him/her self, or is merely reactive to the immediate sensory information of its living, a mere survival machine without idea or thought and therefore incapable of thinking-through life. So even as we know that the self is a convenient composite of various and multiple processes, we cannot ultimately dispose of it. We can re-configure our relation to it, but we cannot dispose of it. We don't build a life, life builds us, but it is advantageous for the entity that he/she believes that they do. Thus, the parenthetical self is something of a coping mechanism, a simple way to process the vast, dissonant pattern of information generated by the body in its relation to the world. Convenient shorthand for this relation, the self proves evasive even as we try to locate it. And placing our selves in the ephemeral now merely short-circuits any possibility of cognitive advancement: lacking both future and past, consciousness defaults to simple animalistic conduct. We become mere survival machines.

It is not anyone's fault that we have come to equate consciousness with selfhood, especially as this has become the spiritual attachment we call the soul. Each and every social system has evolved some variant of the self as a spiritual component, the homuncular phantom that haunts and controls the body. Can we fault anyone for this? Even as evidence contrary to it becomes more available to us, we still assume this, assume a degree of primal inference, conjecture and the simplistic rationalizations formed from available and superficial evidence. Being as we are and present, as the construct of self is only available to us as it is a function, we assume a complete and continuous ontology and from this draw fault (y) lines of association that lead to the belief in the phantom self.

We are not expected to know the truth, nothing in our evolution directs us towards it, and quite often we ignore the truth if it proves detrimental to the course of subsistence and survival evolution directs us towards.

The conceptual mind that flourishes within the frame of the unstoppable cognitive process, encouraged and developed through the cycles of feedback thought initiates and the subsequent amplification of those thoughts into more complex realizations, feeds both the factual and the counterfactual: all things are considered, even as they might be false.

In addition to the variations of the self/soul construct that are prolific with most religions, there is the odd suspicion of the conceptual mind that most of them share. The mind is seen to be unfocused, and by being unfocused it prevents us from both experiencing the now and straying from a "true course" set by moral considerations. This rejection of the conceptual mind equates the randomness by which thought is engaged with a certain lack of discipline. Reining in the mind is seen as bringing us closer to the truth of our existence and therefore securing a level of peace.

But of course it does! It brings us back to the functional, the subsistence environment of the survival machine. This quasi-mystical exhortation of "being in the now" through the halting of the conceptual mind is the confusion of the primal "instinct" and the simplistic inference structure for the seemingly "advanced" mode of inner peace. And it certainly is as it merely shuts down the conceptual function of cognitive processes, resulting in an existence marked by function and not by progress. Now personally, I enjoy the conceptual mind, and I believe we have all benefited from it, even as I feel I am burdened with the "I". But there is no either/or here: to be conceptually engaged means sacrificing the "present" ("being-in-the-now") for the cognitive faculty of temporal extension; being capable of thinking through past, present, and future. To obtain the occasional flashes of insight we must be willing to tolerate, simultaneously, perpetual rounds of petty and burdensome thought as well as the burden of the "I".

The thing is, you can't do both at the same time: you can't be in the now and you can't extend into time (past/future) simultaneously. We alternate between the two. Yes, they exist simultaneously, but are at covariance. You can't enter, aware and conscious or experienced, either stream at the same time: it is either one or the other given the limitations of our condition.

Such is the blessing of our shortcomings; we can jump between them, by virtue of our consciousness, but cannot occupy both.

The burden of self along with the occasional insight: you cannot engage conceptually without A) spatial and temporal extension and B) possessing a construct of the self (because conceptual mind is contingent on the presence of the construct of the self). This give-and-take, the result of, and resulting in, the formed consciousness amplified from the initial conditions (call them primal or whatever), cannot be separated. They are synchronous. And they are necessary.

I know it seems odd and contradictory to challenge both the existence of the self, negating the conventional homunuclar, to postulate its necessity. The challenge then is both: the self does not exist as the known and static persona, the phantom self of soul or brain, but as an aggregate and perpetually emergent construct. What would, then, this self be?

Let's be clear about this: I would not state here that self, as a locatable, physical reference does not exist. It is the being of a Self that is questionable, the being of this construct.

We are "some one" but we are not the "being of some one". The Self is a generalization, a convenient categorical reference point, but not a "being."

It might be a "strange loop", as Hofstadter offers. As we are not mere survival machines, like mosquitoes, or ants, or bears etc. etc. but are cognitive, self aware thinking machines, we are capable of accounting for our selves but rarely come to accept the limitations. Something is lacking in the whole process, this taking the good with the bad.

Even then, the term "self" probably is no longer applicable once the revelation of its "atomized" structure sets in. How, then could we distinguish between 'brain', 'mind', 'self' and 'consciousness'? On that, we may first jettison the distinction between 'self' and 'consciousness', which, in this context, pretty much amounts to the same: lacking any sort of confirmable location of a continuous and static "persona", 'self' is consciousness merely by virtue of being conscious of itself. And in that regard, it is involuntary, a process engendered by the brain/mind in its cognitive function. In having already discussed 'self' in this regard, one could thus assume that any previous or future mention implies this involuntary process of a neurological construct. Even while "being no one", our consciousness, self-aware and self-defining, remains. We can be conscious and cognitive without access to self, we can "be no one" without sacrificing our humanity.

The self as identity is, on the other hand, a more voluntary habit; a postulation from sense that something "is there" that is cohesive and continuous. This assumption of inviolable agency, gathered through the inference from superficial evidence, has, as said, evolved/amplified into an actual, reified entity, especially as it is employed in the conduct and definition of persons so designated in the general social system.

This conceit of self as an identity, extending from the substrate consciousness provides, obviously affords us the notion that we are self-same. That self-ness, the 'being some one', must be a fact, because there is reciprocation by which we can depend. Yet, the 'being no one' that consciousness constitutes guarantees no such discernable reciprocation: the rate of alteration in the aggregate and construct of the self-identity that consciousness provides for, is indiscernible, but is still there. This indiscernible passage through time allows for the illusion of a "being someone" that merely seems autonomous, but is, in fact, contingent: the persistence of ego through time but not necessarily through space.

What I would suggest is that there are impedances that prevent us from such acceptance, impedances that, on one hand, are direct by-products of the feedback/amplification development of consciousness and the construction of the self, and, on the other hand (also simultaneous) have congealed into social conventions that are now, themselves, inextricable from our cultural imperative. Three are, I think, the most problematic: identity, as just mentioned, is a voluntary faculty, a conceptual construct that provides the architecture by which we assume a static self that represents ourselves to the world; originality, the notion that what is us is "new", isolated, inviolable, and reliant on nothing other than ourselves; and sentiment, which would be the emotional content that provides the feedback that informs and maintains the self-identity construct.

I could not hope to answer these things, to provide an alternative. But in being aware of the intricacies under which consciousness and society operate and co-mingle, in how Classical notions that inform our perspectives are both inconsistent and incommensurate with how material reality works, we might more efficiently negotiate our way through the world. I have, in the following pages, tried to develop not necessarily "true" accounts of "how things work", but offer a sort-of speculative thought experiment of how they might. Are we seeing things as they really are? Do we truly build a life? Are we even here? Are we each someone? Are we each "no one"? Or are we "no one" being "some one"? This book will not tell you how to build a life the conventional way, but considers the way (a) life appears, how it occurs and from that how we come to believe that it is built, fabricated. I will not pretend here that any notion is orthodox, nor backed by research. It is speculative, departing from previous work and theories that have grown out from them. "Nothing is obligatory, everything is permissible."[3]

Then again, given the flaws and errors that we have, inadvertently, developed into functions, we probably are doomed to the same patterns. The same patterns that will, no doubt, surprise us with the integrity of their future, vertiginous, and exponential, development.

---

[3] pg. 98 *Counterfactuals*, David Lewis, 2008 Blackwell

I Am A Copy of A Copy of A Copy of a Strange Loop

There is this old episode of *Star Trek: the Next Generation* that, and I don't remember the specifics, features a specie whose replication through cloning has resulted in a degradation of genetic code: the specie's process of cloning from a clone of a clone of a clone (ad infinitum, infinite regress) resulted in "reduplicate degeneration": successive generations of copying from a copy had basically damaged the integrity of their genetics. I can't remember what exactly was the result, but my own conclusions, through having engaged in various types of "reduplicate degeneration" of video, audio, photo print processes leads me to think that the specie would inevitably disappear. Copies of copies of copies of copies… inevitably we arrive at a loss of a structural integrity: one can no longer assume or recognize the end result as the figure we began with. Indeed, the end result is its own figure, and no longer a copy of an original (even if barely there).

Try it. Find an old "analogue" Xerox machine or take a pair of old analogue video or audio recorders (I might also add here that A) your recording ought be "ambient", not direct (line-in duplication) otherwise the ambient quality of the sound will not be affected by the acoustics of the environment) B) I have not tried this with digital recording exclusively and would assume that reduplicate degradation would occur, but I don't trust digital because digital tends to secure faithful duplication) and take a shot, an initial "original", then, rather than copying from that original, copy the copy or record the recording. You will instantly see a "breakdown" in the integrity of the image. Now, copy that copy, record THAT recording.

Over a series of successive generations, you will soon arrive at a point where all recognizable qualities of the original will have been removed, arriving at something completely different.

So, if this were to apply to genetic replication not from an original but from a series of copies of copies, inevitably one would assume, that the specie would arrive at a point where it would be unrecognizable, a shadow of itself.

And this could be so, but would probably take forever, considering the variables of time and integrity.

Then again, we have been doing this for a long time; generations of descendents have lasted through a long series of replication and retained structural integrity by introducing different elements, different inputs and genetic conditions. It is not always the copy we are copying from, something else, outside of the genetic code, another, different genetic code, introduces yet again another element that prevents the copy from being a faithful or corrupted copy, an "original" in itself.

Cloning then would succeed as long as we are not cloning from a clone cloned from a clone, but cloned from an original each and every time. Maintaining a degree of integrity in the copy is essential to genetic replication and industrial production, but essential to what?

And what if we extend this? I propose here that everything, particularly in the realm of knowing, thought and cognition, is a copy of a copy… (the ellipsis indicating an indefinite and protracted extension). We are perpetually engaged in a process of reduplication of information, information that is not copied from a singular master, as in industrial production, but copied from previous copies.

Hofstadter, in *"I Am a Strange Loop"* proposes that we are all copy machines, that in our consciousness we are predisposed towards appropriation of elements through a sort of copying mechanism.

Let's start with that, a simple enough "revelation". This is indicative of basic biological processes; the fact that our genetic information is a copy of another set of genetic information, that we start as replicants and continue to do so. But it goes beyond that, becomes far more complex, given feedback and amplitude variables.

But let us be clear, a little more specific: not one thing we copy is from an original source. We are many generations removed from the point of origin, from the original source. We are copies of copies of copies…ad infinitum, which, thanks to the various mechanisms of evolution and adaptation, have maintained a (relatively) consistent biological-structural integrity.

But this condition of duplication, itself an inherited/copied trait, if we allow ourselves to insert "copy" in place of "inherited", extends to many other areas of existence and most particularly in that of consciousness: here we are copies of varying degrees of characteristics and extremes. It is how we know, how we think, how we act. And again, and especially in terms of consciousness, we copy from a copy, not from an original. In fact, we know of no original, only the various generational descendents of copies. We are not just a "culture of the copy", we, individually and as individuals, integrated collectively, are a monstrous Xerox copier, copying the copies so generated.

We first must make a distinction between A) serial replication and B) sequential reduplication. In the following I will attempt to elucidate the distinction through various examples.

Serial replication

Serial replication could be termed that process of production of an item/object that is modeled from an original, produced with the intent to accurately reproduce a multiplicity of versions from a single and original source. Serial replication is initiated from a single and original source, from which all objects copied from are symmetrical and faithful reproductions. From the singular item, you have many similar items of the same. This is typical of mass produced commodities: for example, CDs, dolls, computers, cars, etc. These are accurately reproduced with the intention of fidelity and faithfulness to an original.

For example, with the process of direct, in-line copying I have a photo of a '68 Lincoln Continental:

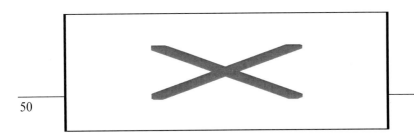

According, first, to manufacturing specifications, every model so made on the assembly line descends from a single "master", from blueprints, diagrams, and mechanical drawings; every car made must be faithful reproductions of the single, master model that the mechanical drawings suggest.

Second, my photo, through the copying mode of my browser, copied from a photo posted on a website, could now be printed and then placed on the glass of a photocopier or scanner.

From this one, single image I can, similar to the manufacturing process that brought this model to the showroom and thus photographed, generate a multitude of nearly exact reproductions.

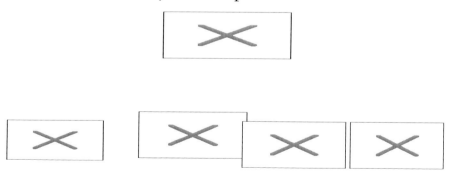

So, from one "master' I generate multiple copies of the same thing, with little variance in the quality of the copies, little loss in the structural integrity of the image.

Serial replication typifies the processes of production and mass communication. It is not reduplicative but duplicative and is intended to multiply chosen objects with fidelity and faithfulness to an original. It is, of course, the process that we are most familiar with, the most pervasive in our consumer culture.

Sequential reduplication

Sequential reduplication, on the other hand, characterizes the process of reproduction from a previous source. There is no attempt at 'fidelity", of a faithfulness to an original. Each descends as a copy from the previous in an infinite regress that frequently results in a corruption of the content. Case in point: photocopying the photocopy. Whereas one would normally duplicate multiple copies from an original, placing the original document on the glass and running off multiple copies, in sequential reduplication one would copy the original, take the original off the glass, and put the copy just made on the glass and copy that, continuing on, copying the copy of the copy.

(Now, whether or not this is an infinite process is debatable, and whether or not we wish to invite the elucidation of an infinite regress, I shall abbreviate the process as *"copy of a copy…"* the ellipsis denoting not infinite regress but regress nonetheless. The point here is not to "wonder" over the infinity that such a process invokes, but to concentrate on the process itself. Personally, we would arrive at a point where the process would exhaust itself and the resulting copy's similarity to previous copies would be negligible.)

The opening section of this book is an example of sequential reduplication, the reduplication of the title page of Hofstadter's "I Am A Strange Loop" through successive (de)generations. The following are as well:

I AM

I AM

I AM

I AM

I AM

I AM

As you can see, the sequential progression through the reduplication of the previous image results in a loss of structural integrity and image fidelity. As a mechanical process, it is only illustrative of that. But as a metaphor for cognition as a way to (albeit in a rudimentary fashion) view the process of information acquisition and retrieval, from the world and from memory, it allows us to witness the progressive action of unconstrained reduplication. In that nothing is acting on the sequence other than the reduplication of the preceding copy, nothing is added and the image is allowed to degrade.

Would, then, a piece of information acquired through cognition also follow this line of degradation? Is information so degraded ultimately corrupted? Not necessarily, information remains information even as the form of it is altered. But given that "corruption" and "degradation" are terms burdened with moral implications, most would certainly recoil at the notion that our cognitive skills are loaded with such seemingly sinister practice!

Yet it seems an essential, innate component of how information is both communicated and acquired. "Corruption" only refers to the loss of fidelity to the preceding quantity, as does "degradation". This does not at all refer here to some of the content, especially as some diabolical influence over it: degraded/corrupted form does not lead to immoral content, just a loss in fidelity. The usual semantic associations of "corruption", "degeneration", and "degradation" with "decay", "depravity", etc. have no relevance here. The processes described have no consideration for moral proclivity, either in action or in conception, and is deferentially indifferent to such considerations. Such moral fabrications exercise an unnecessary burden, making freestanding processes top-heavy and precarious. As it is, reduplication is evolutionary, and even then, evolution is merely reduplicative and, therefore, "corrupts" in that it relies on corruption as a means of progression. I need not mention here that it is not exclusively corruption, that it is also assembly, re-assembly, addition and construction that provide corrections and improvements to guide the evolutionary/reduplicative path.

As it is, then, information, and thus the world, given that the world is information, is infinitely corruptible, at least as it is transmuted through reduplication sequences. And even as the world is infinitely corruptible, it is simultaneously infinitely salvageable and, therefore, constructive.

The following are a series of screen shots from two different videos that have been sequentially reduplicated:

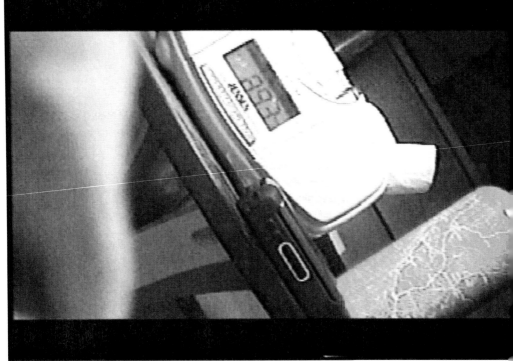
lucid1.JPEG

lucid2.JPEG

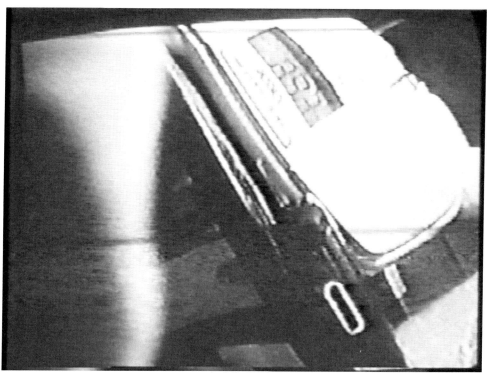
lucid3.JPEG

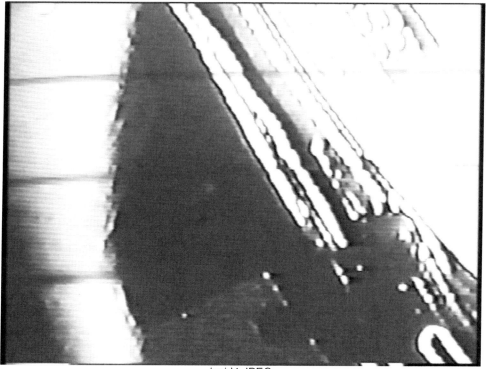
lucid4.JPEG

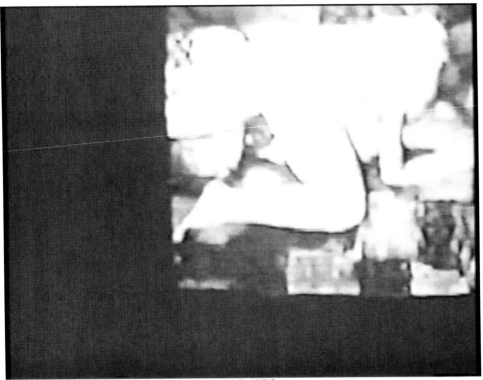
lucid2B.JPEG

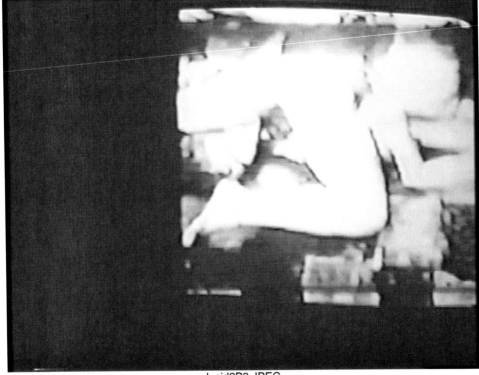
lucid2B2.JPEG

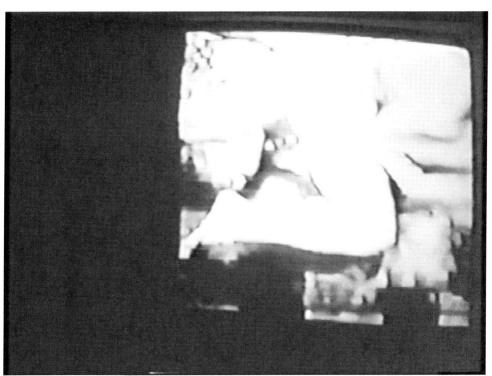
lucid2B3.JPEG

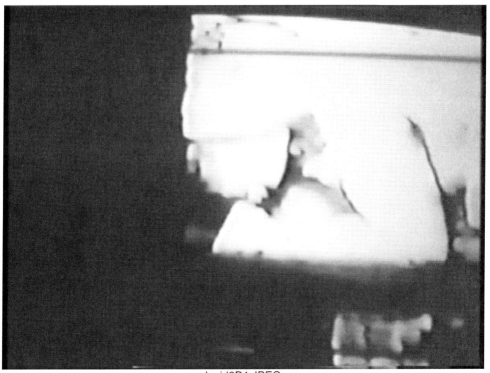
lucid2B4.JPEG

Sequential reduplication might seem an aberration, but on closer examination is far more common and frequent. Thus the lesson from the *Star Trek: Next Generation* episode I tried to recall earlier: inevitably the original content is lost through the degradation of the "original" through reduplication, a gradual degradation into an inevitable, ontological illegibility.

But it doesn't occur, and more than likely, as long as the specie of entities so engaged in such duplication remains in place, it will negligible. Such degradation proceeds at an imperceptible rate, accentuated by processes of feedback and amplification because the sequence is never "pure" in itself, because the process cannot discriminate between desirable and undesirable qualities. In the process, other elements are absorbed, assimilated, making descendant copies original in themselves.

We are not just copy machines; we are *copies* of copy machines.

The process of re-duplication, as subtle, nuanced, and gradual as it is, describes the operation of many processes at varying levels. Certainly this can be employed in the genetic process: we are not serial replicated organisms but sequential reduplicates. We are informed by the genetics of previous organisms that, in turn, were informed by generations of other previous organisms. We might assume that we inherit such information, but as it is not transmitted, nor produced as a signal, it is duplicated in the mode of genetic copying. Genetic information is a copy of a copy and is bound to lose some structural integrity in the process, even as the rate of degenerative loss is imperceptible; rate dictates degree. Generations of re-duplication have not resulted in a final stage of transparency but without a doubt our current genetic make-up is different than the original. Traces remain, small pockets of ancestral information does languish, but are overshadowed by recent additions.

On the level of thought processes, the things of life and thought are not represented nor mirrored in our minds; they are duplicated, copied in the "medium" of consciousness. The copying machine that is our brains, copies data in the medium "natural" to it, which may be neurological "coding", a neuro-code or substrate. Our ideas are not in themselves representations or representative, but duplications, reproductions in the medium of the mind. By way of allegory, take xeroxography: you have toner, light, heat, paper by which you make a copy. In the copying machine of the brain, you have neurological signals, pulses, codes that form the copy. The medium may differ, but the process of duplication remains the same. How we think through things, our ideas of things and other ideas, could be described as, but not limited to, a reduplicative process. Now this would not necessarily be new as offered, for one example, by Hofstadter in "*I Am A Strange Loop*". He proposes just that sort of thing by offering the notion that we are copy machines, but stops short at serial replication. In his analogy, the process of copying is merely a reflexive, representative process in which we simply copy things into our consciousness and deploy them in our cognition of the world. This is fine, but what I propose here is that our copying telemetry is much more involved than simple representative image caching. Leaving us to consider these as 'captures" that leave an imprint in our consciousness, but that they remain there, inviolable and isolated is entirely naïve: from these 'captures' (copies) other imprints are made, and from those imprints others descend sequentially. There is not one imprint but a succession of imprints made from previous imprints. We do not possess the original, nor is, as said, the original accessible. Consciousness functions on sequential reduplication strategies. There is nothing that we know that is in itself original, but descends from reduplication of previous knowledge, thoughts, and ideas.

It is not exclusively sequential, of course. There are functions that require a serial multiplicity and functions that result in sequential reduplication. And even then, nothing attests to a purity of either. First, the reduplicative process cannot discriminate between what is essential and what is superfluous and, second, the rate at which reduplication proceeds varies according to the position of the observer. And being that we are that much closer to it, we cannot perceive the incremental process. Fluidity of reduplication also makes it harder to distinguish what is and what is not "original". We assume the same because the procession is extremely slow. And we can, with confidence, assume the invariable Same without threatening the stability of our comprehension. Difference is by degree, not in kind.

So, much like our genetic process, we engage in a process of reduplication without substantial loss of properties or content. Our "copy of a copy" loop machine provides relatively faithful duplicates with indiscernible flaws. But there are flaws. And the reduplicative process cannot distinguish them as well.

My faulty recall of the *Star Trek: the Next Generation* episode is itself the result of an imperfect copy-of-a-copy my consciousness is engaged in. Cognitively I summon a memory tag of the episode, a brief generalization. But my recall of the episode is copied from a content that is itself a copy of another content. I have tried to copy, not recall, the episode. And my copy is itself a copy of a copy I have attempted to engage with before.

Memory is not only flawed, but as a copy-of-a-copy, it carries the flaw with it, only to be included in the present and future reduplication. My own recall contributes additional flaws as I attempt to "copy" it so that I might communicate it. And, subsequently, you will have copied this communication, imprinting not only my flaw on the copy I provided but your own flaw in the copy you make. You will add something and subtract something that will further degrade the integrity of the so-called original. At no point is the original included. If that where the case, the communication would be a precise, verbatim re-telling of the episode. But, such verbatim is impossible. Even in the engagement with the original, consciousness directs the copying, adding and subtracting even as the original is perceived. And if the "copying machine" that is our consciousness has, say, a flaw in a component, that copy will have included that flaw as well. It should also be mentioned here that this process is not to be confined only to flaws. There are enhancements, additions and subtractions that can make our copies "clear'. But primarily, I think, the underlying process is one of degradation, degradation that is both, and simultaneously, positive and negative. It, of course, requires altering our standard connotations regarding the term "degradation" to either include a positive action or render it more neutral. Degradation is not always sinister, and that would be difficult to overcome given the usual cultural-semantic associations. Briefly glossing over the connotative, the usual employment of the term is in regards to negative human conditions, and my employment here is not to emphasize such negativity (humiliation, a "way of life without dignity") but to explore it as a more "neutral" process, one that is equitable with a process attributed to nature, that is: erosion. The movement of material through addition and subtraction forces an alteration of the topography of a given thing subjected to it. Erosion alters through displacement and removal, but not through deletion. Even as an object is degraded, nothing is removed, not entirely. Even as the copy of a copy moves further from the original, there is some portion that remains.

The same wearing away of the same results in a difference, whether that be of content or appearance, a difference that enables distinction is the result. A river that, in becoming "older" bends into the surrounding landscape until the flow establishes a "path of least resistance" and breaks off from the bend, leaving an oxbow lake. Now, no longer part of the river, it becomes its own body of water. The degradation of the soil embankments, the gradual erosion of the soil, allows for the break and subsequent abandonment. A "new" lake is formed from the displacement of the soil.

In other cases, rain erodes a surface, displacing the material, and degrading the initial surface until a new structure results.

In no way is sequential reduplication erosive, but the pattern of degradation is similar: the displacement of material results in new constructs. In the copy of the copy… the loss of information varies between the negligible and the substantial, but an alteration in its structure is evident.

Let's re-start with a generalization: everything is a copy of a copy…. Such a generalization can be made to account, here especially, only for a few events and situations:

1) Human cognition and thought content
2) Genetics
3) Communication
4) Human/social conduct

Of course, it would have minimal application to anything outside of these realms, like that of astrophysics and such, but parallels can be drawn. It is, by no means, the only process at work in the world, but it is a process that extends through every process at work, not necessarily making it primary, but at least effective and pervasive. But my business here is to concentrate on the above. It is my intention to stay within, and address, these fields.

If everything is a copy of a copy… how do we distinguish one from another? How is difference maintained? How and why do we differentiate between copies? How do subsequent copies appear both "original" and/or "faithful"? Venture three principles:

A) There is just enough "new" information and other variables to distinguish one from another (even the lack of information in one is enough to distinguish it from another, and this lack qualifies as "new information").
B) The integrity of the elements is sound enough to make it relatively resistant to corruption and degradation.
C) Every copy as, by degrees, a variation on the previous, maintains parameters that are peculiar to it, but by no means inviolable.

Degradation, as I have put forth, is one aspect of the process/project of sequential reduplication, and a term whose "sinister" connotations we must separate here. The other term, also applicable here but which we must also remove the usual "sinister" connotation is "corrupt"; "corrupt" may be more exact in its applications, but in employing it, we need to be shed of the moral paradigm that burdens it.

The definitions of "corrupt" as it applies to reduplication, are:

1) "unusable because of the presence of errors that have been introduced unintentionally"

2) "containing undesirable changes in the meaning or errors made in copying"

Dismissing, then, the diabolical, these changes may not be "undesirable" but unintended. And in that little control can be maintained over the process, it is debatable that any such copy could be deemed "unusable". Statements of purpose would have no bearing here, things are as they are and reasons for an entity or event have no application as to why or how they exist. Most importantly, as to the history of the sequence, nothing human's plan is intentional from the start but discovered as it develops, well after the fact of their origin. The sequence of reduplication is one of gradual corruption, neither sudden nor critical. In that we have little access to the original, as what presents itself before us is many times removed from it, we cannot with any certitude ascertain its fidelity. Yet corrupted, as it is, whatever this "it" is, or was, we must assume that, in general, and by the resemblance to what we assume to be the original, it is equivalent. The photo collage demonstrates the gradual corruption of the original, leaving few referential points of direct correlation to the original. We are left to contend with the final, and not the original, and in contending with it, we find ourselves admitting it into the realm of thought, regardless of the degree of resemblance it has or retains. Now as it is, I would like to extend the process/procession of sequential reduplication to experience and to thought, or how thought content is generated and re/de-generated. How is such a process employed in making thought? How is it employed in experience?

First off, everything in consciousness, of ideas and thoughts, are themselves copies of another copy, copies of varying degrees of corruption.

This doesn't make it bad, only different. And difference here is registered only by degrees, not essentially in kind, although it is experienced as being 'in kind'. "For this knowledge plainly rests upon the subject's knowledge of the identity-conditions of the object through time, as well as his knowledge of what it is for an object to possess the property."[4] I have, of course, copied this from pg.111 of Gareth Evans "Varieties of Reference" and for the most part, it is a faithful copy/quotation. And through time I will be able to reference it so.

Evans, of course, cannot now, nor in the future, be held accountable for any corruption of subsequent copies I or my readers might generate. The contingencies of reduplicative fidelity regarding identity-content neither guarantee continued fidelity or guard against subsequent corruption. My copy might appear as a facsimile of his idea, but it becomes its own "original" faithful to itself.

For, in another sense you are not making copies, you are generating originals. Our mental construct of "original" is tenuous, we assume that the original appears unadulterated and

---

[4] Pg. 111, Gareth Evans, Varieties of Reference, 2002 Oxford

inviolable, but that is not the case. As every copy is a corrupt copy of an original, every copy is itself an original. Whether or not it is itself faithful to another has little bearing on this quality. The procession of copies maintains their own identity: they all become their own "original" even as they corrupt what properties they descend from and the corruption that occurs in what descends from them.

In particular, thought and ideas, the whole range of cognitive processing that results in ideas that are either "new" or developed, elaborated, or merely improvised. Dismiss first the notion of mimesis, that pure recording of events, experiences, ideas, and communication through mimicry or representation. That would of course have bearing on our constructs of reality, of how we relate to things and ideas, but none are truly "pure" recordings. We don't purely imitate or represent: there is always some flaw, some corruption that, 1) the limitations of our cognitive parameters impose upon information and 2) occur through the transference of information regarding events and our cognition of them.

Cases in point: if one has, say, some flaw in our vision that impairs our vision, say a cataract, this flaw will effect our perception of a thing or an event, thus effecting the image and memory we have of it. We always attach some personal meaning to events, a meaning that imposes a psychological import that impairs our recollection or the information regarding said event: the psychosexual content related to a fetish object is not inherent in the object itself, nor the information we normally, by convention, have of it, but is something we attach to it.

What could be proposed here is that representation is not the mode by which we accomplish cognition, but replication and reduplication. It is not through mimicry, nor reproduction and representation, that we process information, it is by duplication, reduplication and replication. Case in point is the medieval notion that the mind "mirrors' nature, that we reflect the world in our minds a notion that has been rendered unsatisfactory, despite the persistence of it, its staying power not as a truth but as a tenet of folk psychology. Contrary to this, for consciousness, there is no "reflecting" components, but copying components that also reflect, or, reflecting and reproducing components that are dominant. It is not a "mirroring" that typifies (epi)phenomenal neural components, but a process/processing of components through copying, copying of other copies, copying from the same copy.

So, our mental copy of said object would carry the psychosexual information we have imposed upon it and subsequent copies we would make of that copy would carry that information, alternatively corrupting said previous copy and creating a new entity, an original. Memory is certainly not exempt from this process: all memory is primarily a copying sequence that replicates information as it assimilates and attaches other information. Memory is a copy, we sample from copies of our past and copy them, then copy them again, making them over in variations contingent on the flaws and attributes we attach to them. Some memories are replicated into oblivion, others into entirely different memories that have little resemblance to the "actual", original event or the initial memory we have. Again, this is neither bad nor good, just different.

In fact, the entire process of differentiation is alternatively faulty and precise; the copy is both its own and a copy, an original, but the "same". "Same difference", that odd formation of the

English lexicon, paradoxical in its input, but expressive of the exact position any copy is found in, whether serial replication or sequential reduplication: the copy is different and is its "own" but is simultaneously the same as any other copy, of the original from which it originates. Is it the same water? It might as well be, that is: in many instances the difference is negligible.

This seemingly contradictory condition of the copy would seem to negate its reliability, but that isn't necessarily so. If anything, the 'same difference' of its status would ensure that the content remain actionable as its deployment deemed for it. In the world of the copy, the excluded middle is itself excluded: true and false, negation or affirmation have limited bearing on its employment. Is it true or false? The answer would be "yes", that is because both are imprinted on the copy. What is important is the form of its employment: here form defines function.

In the realm of consciousness and thought, the process of reduplication offers both improvement and corruption. The addition of information or deletion of superfluous information refines and elaborates the ideas expressed, the basis for our improvisations and improvements of previous ideas. The deletion of information or the addition of superfluous information corrupts, but remains a vital point in the generation of copies, a necessary link towards complexity or exhaustion. But even then, we never arrive at a complete erasure of the information involved, only a displacement. Or, we may never arrive at such a point, and if we did, we may never know it.

In a nutshell, then, the general overview here is that the mind, being a copying machine, reaches for a sample of information and copies it. This much is understood, and this much is what Hofstadter et al have formulated. But what I am proposing here is that while the mind is engaged in its copying process it is limited to information that is itself a copy of a copy…. No sample is a "pure representation" nor is it a "faithful' reproduction of an "original". In the realm of this reduplicative machine, no item exists as a result of serial replication. Although the copies can, themselves, exists in serial and multiple processions, they are not arrived at through serial replication. For Dennet's "multiple drafts" model of consciousness, for instance, one would have to admit that the drafts are themselves copies of copies…. We do not appropriate items, information, and information about items as pure facsimiles, but appropriate and generate this information as copies of copies….

Adulterated content would then seem to be rampant in our neurological programming, and subsequently would extend into the social network. How 'things' (the general classification of everything sensible and/or generated through thought) have come to be what they are is, as well, explainable to some degree through sequential reduplication. Entities and agents, engaged in expressing ideas and committing actions that are replicative of other ideas and actions, generate and appropriate through a far wider network of dissemination. This broadened network of reduplication further subjects these "things" into a cultural modeling that entities and agents may or may not choose from.

Whether they are free to do so is not the question here, albeit that it isn't necessarily "freedom" nor "free will", but the various contingencies that determine the process of selection and what is, or can be, selected.

Within any cultural milieu, sequential reduplication functions simultaneously with serial multiplicity. Where, as a cultural function, we generate and disseminate objects, information, and information about objects, through serial multiplicity, simultaneously we are generating and appropriating said objects and information through sequential reduplication. In culture, as in the mind, everything is a copy of a copy... even as it is produced as a copy from an original.

There is nothing exemplary or strategic about sequential reduplication, because, as it is, it is involuntary. There is nothing intentional about it. To ask, to request that components that are directed by and through sequential reduplication should "focus" or direct with precision and exclusion would be inherently impossible.

And the process cannot discriminate between superfluous and essential, truth and falsehood. Anything within the range of the process will be included within the event.

To expect it do otherwise would be wrong. We can, of course, produce a "new object" from serial multiplication, the primary mode of classical production, but subsequent copies would be from that item or entity so produced.

Here Comes the Strange Loops...Or Not....

The principle is nowhere represented in the program; it emerges from the way the program works. [5]

  The question "How did I get here?" is answered simply enough: copulation, insemination, transfer of genetic information, gestation, etc. We understand that. And, as it is, simultaneously we are both the product of serial replication, the organic production of a single organism, and a product of sequential reduplication, that is: a copy of a copy.... Our DNA is replicated from the partners who contribute to our being, information that is itself combined and replicated from previous partners.

---

[5] pg. 261, Phillip Johnson-Laird, *Mental Models*, 1983 Harvard

Genetics is a sequential reduplication process, a copy of a copy… Extending exponentially into a multitude of descendents, recombinant information establishes the patterns of differentiation that curbs inevitable degradation. Copies of copies… here none are pure copies because the pattern so established ensures that the descendent copy gain enough from the recombined information to establish a "uniqueness" on one hand and a fidelity that secures the line of descent.

If it were not for this addition of recombinant information, there would be an exhaustion of replicated information over time. The flaws and deletions/additions once secure the original form and content but makes it vulnerable to a corruption that results in flawed information being communicated to the descendant, thus the varieties of genetic conditions of the human specie, the wide disparities between individuals regarding health, intelligence, lifestyle, etc.

Whereas descendant genetic reduplication of the same information would inevitably result in a loss of fidelity, it does not. Enough variation in the information, through recombination of precursor information, results in a survivable pattern that generates differentiated information, not preserving fidelity to the precursor but the combination generates a differentiated entity, an "original".

What matters, of course, is survivability of information. Repeated cycles of reduplication of the very same information ultimately renders much information degraded, but information that is imprinted with just enough differentiation renders survivable information.

This seems simple enough; a basic, organic template for replicative processes and even then by extension for sequential reduplication, an involuntary function that is neither dominant nor central to the transfer and transmission of information, but underwrites all informational processes. Comparatively, yes, the analogy drawn between electronic copying processes and genetic replication is not exact, but is complimentary. How, then, we get from the "small lumps" of DNA and chromosomes to the self that we become is then, another matter, but yet the same matter, entirely.

Is there a genetic program for transmission of information that is itself replicative? Do we "repeat" the fundamental process of replication in all things we think, say, and do? Quite frankly, I think a case could be made for this, that our neural and cognitive processes follow a similar track that is informed by this basic organic template. Copying (serial replication) is natural enough to us, but is sequential reduplication? And I would argue, bracing for your objections that it is indeed.

There is a bottom>up emergence involved, that a process located on the microscopic level would direct patterns and connections made at the macroscopic level, that is: organic replication would direct the patterns of our thoughts and behavior.

That this could be true is not that far fetched. Is it the semantic content of our ideas that directs behavior and thought or is it grammatical structure? Not everything results in semantic content, nor can we always make clear lines of association that are themselves semantic but appear more grammatical, syntactic. Our lives are not narrative constructs until after the fact. And meaning always evades us even as we construct it.

It has been offered, as Mr. Hofstadter offers in an aside to another publication, that the atomic structures of matter dictates behavior and conduct, that we somehow follow the patterns, in bottom>up emergence communication and direction, of atoms. And this is quite possible (but that the shortcomings of human cognition would prevent us from recognizing this would be conceivable), and it wouldn't really surprise me. I would argue that, not knowing how extensively quantum mechanics would direct quotidian behavior, does not exclude the possibility that it does (and does explain so much of life and living), and by extension, lays out the possibility that grammar would also be affected by micro-level patterns. And, by further extension, grammar would have far greater bearing not only on the formulation of meaning, but also in how we think and how we behave.

Now, I feel, again, that I must make one more cautionary "disclaimer" here: my considerations of reduplication as an essential aspect of human conduct and cognition should not be seen as arguing for it's autonomy and, in no way, a dominance.

In introducing the concept (or reiterating the conccpt) of reduplication, it must be remembered that the concept is tied into the multiplicity of components and processes that direct our behavior and cognition. It is far more complex, but not that complicated I suppose, but I am arguing that in all this, reduplication is a key, albeit neglected, "ingredient", but not the only one. We also must figure in how other components work simultaneously with it and others, especially feedback, amplification, simultaneity, parallel distribution, etc. The multitude of processes operate coextensively with and against each other, and from this point I could not really consider any of them without also integrating the other components in the discussion. (Although it might be argued that these components cannot be apprehended individually anyway, or, in a superposition of processes, cannot be apprehended collectively, leading to the flawed conclusion that one excludes the other, given our inability to comprehend the superpositionality of the various constructs).

The previous mention of both our genetic origins through reduplication/recombination and the grammatically organized behavior hint towards exactly what this conversation initiates: in the emergence of patterns and processes from initial, micro-level complexities.

How do we get from the genetic information, from the grammatical, to the "fully realized" world and self that inhabits and negotiates that world? If I were to say "sequential reduplication" I would be lying, or simply favoring a concept I have some predilection for. And it is not just that, it is a convergence of reduplication, recombination, feedback, and amplification. If it were not for any of these, self and world would remain merely molecular. If it were only reduplication, we would be mere tissue paper, flimsy degraded copies incapable of negotiating through the world.

First of all, reduplication on its own is a sequential degradation of the entity, if left unchecked or left unabated or, most significantly in human social interaction, assisted in its unabated reduplication by interests who require the rigidity of doctrine (that would, of course, actually be a case a serial replication, I suppose, but the rigidity of doctrine insists on faithful reduplication even as it is replicated, regardless of the degradation the doctrine is subjected to, I mean, to levels that exhaust its semantic impact and reduce it to mere syntactical reflection. But that is another matter.)

I suppose this could go one of two ways: as a reduction of the seemingly continuous form to discontinuous elements or as a rigidity that falls into a predictable pattern that reiterates only itself and nothing else, or the nothing of itself. Both can be accomplished through the reduplicative strategy proposed here, the long and lengthy advance through successive and sequential reduplication.

Let me reiterate: it is a copy from the previous copy, not of a master, 'singular' original. As it is progress, it is also evolutionary, both in strategy and employment. The stasis of doctrine, although traceable to a static and rigid reduplicative sequence, could be attributed to the lack, both enforced and unintended, of "exterior" information. Retaining and remaining in a closed loop, even if it is sequentially reduplicated, results in a stultified, stagnant, insular and concentrated comportment.

As you can see, we are leading into an exploration of loops and looping, so it would be important to differentiate between loops (not yet admitting to Mr. Hofstadter's 'strange loop').

Tight loops result in predictable patterns, loops that remain exclusive, self-referential and recursive only of elements native to it regulated through negative feedback

Broad loops result in greater variation, probabilistic as tight loops, but with greater potential. They are inclusive; they draw in greater information and employ this information to initiate new and other patterns. They are more generative, versus self-sustaining and therefore primarily positive feedback loops.

Again, let me reiterate that both rely on sequential reduplication, it is only that the tight loop can be seen to negate expansion through the steady exclusion of extraneous information, that is, it denies information that might affect it. And not all of this is voluntary. In the realm of ideology, tight loops are active and voluntary. In the realm of caste systems, tribal ethos and such, tight loops are resilient. In the realm of behavior, though, involuntary tight loops dictate limits to both behavior and cognition. I cautiously propose that animals, given the limits of their cognitive abilities and that expansive cognitive ability is counter-productive to their essential mode of survival instinct, operate within tight loops, reduplicative (and heavily so), both in their comprehension of space and experience of time and, especially, their memory of both. Indeed, these loops are of short duration and require constant refreshment. An animal, it seems to me, cannot recall one minute from the next (I think of my cats, in which I see this odd inability to remember anything!), and can only do so through the tight and stultified repetition of behavior. Every minute is a constant struggle to ascertain coordinates from the environment that bear on survival. Long-term memory is sacrificed for survival programming.

It is all, I suppose, a lot like the movie "Groundhog Day" that, if you remember, is a series of tight loops of temporal experience with each return distinguished by the slightest degree of variation. That there is a difference between the subjective experience of time ('lived time') and objective "actual time" would have some bearing on all this, and broader loops would of course, by inclusion without discrimination, allow for greater variation. Acknowledging the cyclical dynamic of lived time, by which I mean that subjective assessment of temporality that differs from person to person and moment to moment, who's to say that on some basic level there isn't a reduplicative dynamic in time itself? And even then, the return of the familiar, the repetition of the same, guarantees and secures coordinates on which we can rely upon, if by that we assume reliability in the environment and our cognitive construct (and I would think that the ability to do so would be necessary for our own survival programming!). Whether or not reliability can be a consideration is not at question here, but will be.

Taking the premise of the previously mentioned movie that even time is subject to looping would not exactly bring anyone comfort, but certainly if time were allowed to reduplicate itself without variation, inevitably even time itself would exhaust the elements that compose it. That it doesn't is a relief, certainly, but even then, whose to say? Taking account of lived time rarely coordinates, on a one-to-one ratio, with actual time. Even if actual time did not traffic in loops, our lived time does. And, as it is, time is at once a homogenous continuum until it has been brought into a loop, and when so brought in time is then experienced as heterogeneous and discrete. Removing the mediation of lived time might expose us not to time as loops, the return of the same, but merely as a homogenous, glacial continuity of neither the same nor of difference but of an undifferentiated sludge. There would be no "return" because there would be no departure.

In a tight loop experience, there would be minimal distinctions made from one moment to the next, all the while employing a reduplicative strategy that, on this level of spatial reference, is entirely referential in motivation. And lacking a broader arc in the loop, one would not have access to information that would inform us of our position in time, especially if our cognitive powers were focused primarily on our position in space, such as the survival instinct would command.

This is not to say that a tight loop is exemplary of stupidity, it is just basic, redundant and, therefore, primal. The more repetitive and redundant the loop, the more repetitive and redundant the behavior, and the closer we are aligned to the primitive. The reliance on repetitive behavior and communication, say, with the dog's abbreviated vocabulary, or the tribal routine of hunt/eat, is indicative of tight loops and an alignment with base function. It is subsistence cognition on one level and primal as a point of origin. And, of course, in the human, the tight loop evolves into broad loops through feedback and amplification.

Within the tight loop, there is never a return because there is never a departure within the loop itself. All information is contained as it pertains to spatial position and actions required within it. Extraneous information is excluded as being irrelevant to the requirements of spatial/survival negotiations. The feedback is on a short leash, you might say, the duration of the feedback required for the tight loop is short, with immediate returns that result in a stability, and yet a paucity, of information.

It is, maybe not, clear that duplication is central to it, and I would propose here that reduplicative mechanics are also central (you can't really have one without the other). The duplication of information in the tight loop is primarily spatial, as with sonar on radar, the feedback extends only to those points that inform position and therefore instruct as to required or appropriate action. "I am here, I need to be there...." Initial information is then "copied" but the duration of that copy is brief, subject to decay and/or fading of the quality and clarity of that information. Subsequent copies of that information are already corrupted, so become unreliable and need to be constantly refreshed.

The tight loop scenario is, of course, our primary point of departure in terms of evolutionary cognition, being that loop which informs instinct. This is, of course, where we start, it is the base of cognition in that it is a direct, habitable format for survival and for processing information pertinent to that survival. It is the tight loop that forms the basis for the broad loop. So from the tight loop, what accounts for the "leap" into the broad loop?

Tight loops are never far removed from the function of broad, strange loops. They run parallel to them, even as they are subsumed. The lock of the tight loop enables referential patterning that draws in duplications of the self-same information but excludes information extraneous to this. The self-referentiality of the tight loop is primarily focused upon the referentiality of the information.

But the broad loop, running parallel to the tight loop, initiates the complex of self-referentiality beyond the redundancy of information. At some point, the tight loop stumbles, say, opening itself to the inclusion of extraneous information and initiating true self-referentiality. Somehow, the tight loop of the brain-stem function becomes self-aware, or allows for self-awareness. It is at that instant that feedback, normally held to the stability of the self-same, amplifies into an initial broader arc: suddenly the tight loop is aware of itself, or produces an event where it becomes aware of itself as itself.

Now this isn't an account of a sudden, primal "enlightenment", the attainment of cognitive nirvana that initiates the leap from animal to human; it is as we know reliant on a number of factors that ran parallel to this development, events that made both the tight loop and the broad loop possible. And it is conceivable that these "evolutionary" developments, in terms of brain size, neurological development, were themselves products of genetic looping, the feedback of genetic information forcing alterations and improvements in the organs of cognition and knowing.

Underlying all this is the machinations of the reduplicative process, this machine that is not only copying the information required for its development but also copying copies of this information. The reduplicative loop tends to broaden the sweep of the loop, or forces such a broadening as it assimilates and replicates information in both feedback of reference and the amplification of the sweep. It makes possible the extension of thought into space and time: we can now anticipate future events through the construction of scenarios, we can "place" ourselves in the future, we can think not only of ideas, but about ideas, we can think through our environment as well as think through thought itself.

How we "got here" is certainly explainable in (fact) of genetics and copulation and (fiction) of myth, but how we "stay here" in terms of how we become our Selves is explainable, it seems, only either through the (fiction) of myth (itself a product of budding broad loops), or the speculation of neuro-cognitive studies. And in terms of what I am discussing here, where this might lead is to the following proposal (much in keeping with Mr. Hofstadter's thesis); the broad loop is an essential component of the construct of Self. Not only the strange loop of self-referentiality, and the tight loop of spatial reference, but the broad loop of reduplicative stratagems, the ability to process and recombine information from the environment (social systems and cultural systems) and from information generated through the 'internal' mechanism of cognition. The Self is not only a loop of information, amplifying itself with each sweep of the loop into a broader array of elements and functions, but is itself a copy of a copy….

With sequential reduplication, that the concern is less with fidelity but with re-generation of information is the entire basis for the improvisation of variations between entities. We are not entirely direct copies, nor "faithful". And as with the information itself, the Self as a copy of a copy is an original, even as it is 'corrupted".

But, let me be clear: it is not a sinister corruption, nor is the corruption complete.

Is this, then, an evolutionary process? In the development of man as specie, it could be, and it would be a premise here, not fact, regarding the base level of development. But in regards to the development of human consciousness, it could be a "significant" contribution to the established notions.

Through the parallel combination of broad loops of consciousness, the strange loop of self-referentiality, sequential reduplication, amplification, and feedback, we may have the basis for a continuing theory of how we come to be our Selves, how the "illusion" of being some one, begins and develops.

...OR NOT? *Do loops exist?*

Generally, when working through some theory and the apparatus it is installed upon, we attempt to hold to a premise subscribed to without variance, a certain stubbornness regarding the validity of the premise. But I would be remiss to continue to do so. I suppose that such a break half way into the work is not without precedent, but to keep it here and not alter anything before it, that could be problematic for some.

But one must account for the path, that the break from the accepted patterns should be accounted for. For the notion of loops is sufficient, even as they are about to be excluded.

Loops and the theories applying them are intriguing constructs. And I would also be remiss to out and out dismiss them. They are there, they are there as constructs of thought.

But do they truly "exist"? Do we truly refer to something concrete when we speak of them? Well, we do when thinking of them, as they are a product of thought. But the truth might be, I say *might be*, more tenuous regarding their presence and application. Caustic even, in that loops may actually not be welcomed constructs, even as nothing in and of the world admits to linearity, we might not be able to locate loops.

To conceive at this point a model of consciousness that dispenses with looping seems unheard of, heretical. What it might be is; they don't loop, they bend.

The sporadic and tenuous appearance of loops in consciousness and experience is explainable only as a trick of perspective and the shortcomings of cognitive processing. Indeed, we might also be approaching an event that is inviolable as it occurs but violable as it passes. We assume that the passing of a signal requires a return in some way because we cannot conceive of any other pattern, nor could we process any other pattern. The example of the amplified speaker feedback, a guitar resting against an amp and suddenly squealing from the recursiveness of the electronic signal, is a fine metaphor, but I wouldn't say that it qualifies as a loop: there is a point of satisfaction, a point of saturation that, even as the information is not in itself stable, is the point of stability of the amplification. No, it won't bring down the house, but it will not, in itself, arrive at a musical structure. What seems to be a loop is merely the point at which the feedback is amplified, sending the trajectory not into itself but out into a spiral and finally settling into a distinguishable pattern, a leveling.

So let me venture a break from the standard issue: there are no loops. Or, more to the point, there are no loops in consciousness and experience even as we construct them, that even as we admit to them they are not there. Or they are not there until we admit to them. (And, I suppose, this would be the way that I would have my cake and eat it, too. That I can simultaneously allow for and dismiss loops.) In general, the duplicative/reduplicative mechanism is in place, and confusing the corrupt copy for a stable loop is probably the rule, not the exception. The inability to admit to and to admit loss, separation, erasure is attributable to the insufficiencies of consciousness, a shortage in the capacity to assimilate what is not present or what is no longer present.

I would admit that, given that loops exist as structural components, constructs of mathematics, topology, physics, it would be too hasty to jettison them. Questionable is the long-term relevance of their employment as definers of cognitive processing, they would essentially have relevance to cognitive development, but are not descriptive of it. Loops present themselves at nascent levels, they are preliminary structures and structuration, they allow for development of cognition, self and identity, and even genetic/organic development. They are developmental, progressive auto-constructs that enable development of the various constructs but are not representative of the construct themselves. They are a part of the mechanism but are not the mechanism themselves.

And then again, it is difficult to differentiate between what is a loop and what is amplified feedback, which is looping in appearance, especially as experienced from a single perspective, but is primarily spiral in action, composed of partial loops, bends, that return but not in the condition they departed as. Self-affecting, yes, I suppose. But as a loop describes the return of the self-same, in an endless Ouroboros of self-same configuration, the structure required to depict cognitive processing or any other process would not at all follow this topology, but would spiral without return.

Therefore, the contestation is not over the actual existence of loops, but as to their application and relevance. Memory could be described as a loop, but quite often not every point immediately resembles itself. Looping just does not account for deterioration, corruption, assimilation, and accretion.

The topology of amplified feedback, the curl and spiral that also weaves into a network of bends and lines, addresses the situation at which information achieves a point of saturation and thus stabilizes. Once stability is reached, even as it is itself unstable, the assumed loop falls off, no longer required for the development of the process, no longer essential. There is a point where the assumed loop breaks free of itself, copies itself, and by all appearance, no longer resembles itself.

If there was a way to reify the topology of the cognitive distribution, then, we would see that the loop we assume, given the limitations of our cognitive mechanism, the three dimensionality of perception, would actually appear to be a portion of a larger, complex spiral, the bend or curve of a greater network, analogous to the iceberg in the water, or more of the sea serpent whose visible peaks rise above the water level while unseen troughs of its torso sink below, we assume wholeness and inviolability of the parts.

Cognition could then be seen as being distributed along bends, curves and spirals, not loops. Loops assume a discrete and inviolable packet that is entirely self-sustaining, but given that a loop is really only a portion of a larger network, it is only discrete at the point at which it is perceived or experienced. The continuum of information extends further and out then the loop admits. Here come the strange spirals….

From this point going forward, and backward, I must compensate for any mention of loops with the more appropriate notion of a helix. My reluctance to return and correct for this 'sudden realization' has as much to do with my laziness as with the point that nothing already said about loops would be made invalid by the postulate of the helix. The helical construct, a strange helix, does not really refute anything loops offer, but it does explain, maybe, the loss of original information, or its improvement. It may more accurately graph the trajectory of information when a reduplicative component is introduced. The loss or improvement of the features in the copy results in the loss of the original, that it does not return as the same, as it is amplified and stepped further away from the original in the sweep of the trajectory.

And we must also think of multiple helixes, parallel and simultaneous helixes that amplify and defeat, inhibit each other and inhabit the same space.

Nothing then essentially changes: the parameters of tight and broad so described above remain essential for the helical as it did for the loop: helical distribution (and parallel helical distribution) and amplification occur in both tight helixes and broad helixes.

So, what would have been said about tight or broad loops can also be said for helixes, with the exception that nothing would return as the same, nor would it depart as a difference. Information, cognitive and experiential, can only be reduplicated with numerous assignations derived from improvisation. We mark what is original as different and assign the copy to the same, failing to realize that even the original is not itself original.

THE REDUPLICATIVE HELIX

Even then, this might be all we need to know: in Mind, everything is a copy. How it gets there is not our concern. Copying information as bits and pieces and re-presenting them to others and ourselves is an essential mode of cognition. We assume the brain is there to be thumbed through like a "rolodex", that everything of memory is indexed and chaptered, inventoried and archived. Which might not be the case.

What we might assume to be evolution may, in actuality, only be amplification, or feedback from amplification that forms a progressive spiral reaching a saturation point that is itself a tenuous plateau of stability. As a genetic program, the strange spiral of genetic information that describes an entity is itself amplified in its reduplication, spiraling back into past information, characteristics are amplified as they are required while others are subsumed as they are no longer required.

"Although some computer scientists consider a machine that describes itself to be introspective, it can hardly be said to understand itself. It produces complete description of itself that is useful for self-reproduction, but it no more understands this description than a molecule of DNA can be said to understand genetics."[6]

We could view the progress of an organism less as a step-by-step progression and more as a process of helical amplification and reduplication. A specie would be seen as amplifying successful responses and routines, and reduplicating successful characteristics that correspond to them. A specie would not really shed itself of less successful traits and responses but lose them in the process of being reduplicated; lost in

---

[6] Pg. 471, Phillip Johnson-Laird, *Mental Models*, 1983 Harvard. In remembering it, that is, in producing a mental copy of the copy, I assumed (and therefore imprinted) that the thought expressed applied to genetics, that he had written that genetics was description. In finding the actual quote, I was dismayed to find out that I had remembered/copied the intended meaning wrong.

the degradation of copy, what remains is the portions that emphasize themselves, those "hardened" elements that succeed through persistence of pattern. Habits are themselves subject to the rules of survival.

If there are such rules, which could easily be re-written as "survival of the persistent", not necessarily the fittest, and not always ensuring a rational of survival, that is: not every trait or characteristics benefits or guarantees survival, may even be detrimental, as if a pre-determined program for failure. All this is especially true in the world of ideas: not every idea itself secures truth or even relevance, but survives not by virtue of being the "fittest" but only of being persistent. As it is, in the sweep of the reduplicative helix, the process cannot discriminate between the good or bad, beneficial or the detrimental. What "succeeds" can only be arrived at by whatever structural integrity remains of the habit or trait being reduplicated, whether it is suitable or not.

EVOLUTION AS AN AMPLIFIED HELICIAL SEQUENCE

The terms of inheritance imply an obligatory description descended from precursor events and entities: we assume a descendance of traits and instincts from previous models. And not that this is entirely wrong, it is not: amplified helical sequencing is intended to augment evolutionary theory, not detract from it. And though the double helix describes the structure of genetic information, amplified helical sequence in no way mirrors as analogy, it is merely meant to describe the habitual pattern of information in the ascendancy and descendancy of traits.

Evolution theory assumes transference of information as if genetic data was itself sentient, capable of intervention on behalf of the organism by itself. As mentioned, the loop model commonly employed overlooks certain variables and sequencing of the mechanism and subsequent complexity. Self-contained loops often spill over, collapse, and exaggerate traits deemed either advantageous or detrimental. And yet, even in this, information along assumed loop lines do not remain self-similar: there are alterations, upgrades, and loss of integrity, mutations.

So, because information is not always predictably, consistently self-same, returning to its point of origin nearly intact, what explains the loss and gains?

Such loss and gain is explained away in evolutionary theory that traits are distributed over time through their "proof" of their advantage, survival being key to the resilience of tried-and-true traits on one hand and organic features on the other.

Here, we should not be concerned with evolution in terms of the progressive evolution of organisms themselves. Elements, like gills, teeth, tails and such drop off or improve not with advantage itself but in terms of use and employment: neglected parts fall away, frequently employed parts gain favor and are improved upon.

But what we are concerned with here are the neuro-cognitive and psychological traits

that informs socio-cultural conventions, are informed by socio-cultural convention, and inform habits and traditions we personally relate to. Do learned responses inform genetic patterns? Is there a direct line between a person's response and to his/her genetic field?

Only as it is distributed, simultaneous and parallel, but not directly associated. How we "evolve" our conventions from habits and routines cannot always be explained by evolution (or, at least the popular interpretation). Not everything, in terms of traits, instincts, procedures, that 'survives' is clearly advantageous and sometimes detrimental. This would not admit to a certain "strategy" of survival that constructs a progressive pattern of survivability; evolution is blind to intent and moral distinctions.

So, in terms of our "psychology', we pass on and inherit through description and reduplication, but not as an actual evolutionary stage. The feedback associated with regulatory inhibition or enabled action is not always in the form of a self-contained loop and this is particularly true of evolution.

Let us take the current "epidemic" of obesity in America: is this evolutionary in terms of survivable traits that adapt to current circumstances? If this were so, then it speaks only to the blindness of evolution itself, a general indifference to the seemingly "moral".

But as it is a socio-cultural construct, born of learned responses to environment, how did we get here? Certainly not from a simple, self-contained loop of repetitious and self-same information. The evolution here is not a progression from point A to B, nor is it the feedback or feedforward of consistent recursion. Something breaks free of the recursion to amend into something else, into some exaggeration of a previous pattern into a more complex pattern that is distinct from but distinguished. Subtle trajectories of information do not immediately reveal alteration and are, therefore, overlooked. And we would notice them more if they remained the same, stuck in a recursive pattern!

Given that our socio-cultural conventions fail to remain consistent over time, a negligible inconsistency for the most part, but inconsistent nonetheless, our default mechanism of recursive loops does not adequately explain their "evolution". Genetic replication explain the loss and gain of traits, but even then, there are negative traits that persist and positive traits that fall away. Correction is not always correct: the human's diminished capacity for nocturnal vision proves this, even as the interference born of our constructed, illuminated environment explains the diminished capacity.

Something else occurs in the assumed recursive pattern that allows for alteration and mutation. There is a point where recursive patterns escape themselves, turning away from the usual and assumed route of the self-same and becomes "something else". This transformative point has less to do with inheritance and evolution than we would like to admit: we assume inheritance because our perception is of the immediate, equivalent and equidistant, local and not general. The vanishing point of the vast transformation prevents us from seeing its entire pattern. Inheritance explains only the local and immediate.

If we were to look at it from the general, overall perspective, we would not see a recursive loop, but, again, a helical sequence where successor events spiral off and away from precursor events, a gradual spiraling, imperceivable on the level of immediate experience. We "see" the information depart from us but it disappears along the horizon, its return is assumed to be the same, but it is not. Being that it is A) a copy of a copy and B) departed from the "original", the loop collapses as the helical swerve carries it.

What, then, might explain this is the notion of amplification. Helical sequences, even as the incidents and elements may only be reduplications, gain through the amplification of information, or input.

Input is, then, not the same as output and does not recur at the same point. There is a stepping-up with every sweep, every reduplication. We assume a loop, as said, because we cannot see the points of return and departure.

The socio-psychological helix quantifies information and then "repeats" only the fundamental elements through reduplication and, in the process, amplifies them into successive variations, difference by degree, not in kind. We recognize the similarity but do not realize the difference because the process is subtle, gradual. The information "seeks" the route of similar and self-same patterns, but can never really return to them, even as it seemingly returns, it "departs" different, i.e.: amplified.

In evolution, genetic information is not so much inherited, but augmented, edited and amplified. We carry the description of ourselves that is A) a copy of a copy of a copy…prior to us and B) that even then, discrete bits are discreetly amplified into different "shades", or discreetly deleted. Either way, a change occurs that, ultimately, is insignificant in itself, as an information event. It is only the accumulation of such events that proves significant in the long run. This is, of course, not to say that inheritance does not exist, it certainly does and specifically in terms of biological development of the specie. But as to the extra-genetic traits that the descriptions DNA makes possible, the extensions of biological components, amplification compliments, providing the impetus for development of such things as cognition, consciousness, and dexterity. But more so, amplification is especially evident in socio-cultural development. What I propose here is not at odds with any such interpretation, and as one might see a contradiction, or a lack of clarity in my support of sequential reduplication and amplification as essential components in human consciousness and socio-cultural development, I heartily disagree: all these "forces" compliment each other. I don't think it is my place to "choose", simply to speculate.

A Pause for a Preemptive Summary…

So, as proposed here for the model employed, the helical sequence, elements described for loops, broad and tight, still have application. And in that no single helical routine dominates but performs through and in association with others, we aren't describing a linear, concentric progression but a complexity of various differential sequences, tying into, binding, and dissembling into one another.

Given the native deficiencies of normative and normalizing cognitive processing, due to the latent shortcomings of the organism and its organ of cognition, the brain, we cannot see the whole of the pattern and only the parts most immediate or reduplicated through lateral chains of communication.

The helical sequence does not exclude feedback even as it is not the return of the same or similar information; feedback still serves to regulate and guide both incidental and coincidental progress, but occurs along the trajectory at discrete intervals. And these intervals are simultaneously reduced or amplified depending on the degree of attention or employment allowed them. In genetics, each inherited trait is an amplification of elements leading to the next sweep in the helix, or a loss of information due to lack thereof. In cognitive development and the construct of the self, the same applies: development is achieved through the amplification or muting of information through employment or attention or lack thereof (and even then, the lack itself can become amplified).

As for amplification, not everything is amplified nor is everything reduced or deleted; variance in amplitude leads to exclusion or pronunciation, muting or amplification. Some elements 1) lend themselves to amplification by being, favorably or unfavorably, pronounced or 2) some are brought in inadvertently or 3) some are neglected and 4) some are only partially amplified, remaining as schematic "ghosts".

Is, then reduplication compatible to amplification? They are, but more, are really the same thing: amplification is reduplicative, but reduplication is not always amplification. And as it is, where reduplication maybe a component of genetics, it is far more primary in cognition and consciousness. In fact, one might say that it isn't there until observed.

The Social Turns

As reduplication is active in an entities' neurological amplification of information, amplification is more evident in the socio-cultural processing of information provided by individual human agents, (whom we will now refer to as 'nodes' in that they function as reference points in the matrix of the social-cultural mechanism) and their interactions

It is with each sweep of the helical turn that socio-cultural progress receives acceleration and complexity.

Let us return for a moment to our example of obesity. If the "epidemic" of American obesity serves no genetic purpose in terms of survival, did it become this way? And what possible effect will it have?

Of course, there is the "vicious circle" of a locked feedback loop, the poor choices stemming from poor or limited options (given the craven nature of American food processing of the last century). And as these events are returned, they depart amplified, exaggerated into greater complexity, drawing in and expelling greater amounts of information. The degrees removed from the initial conditions determine both the complexity and the loss of fidelity to those initial conditions, thus the tendency of such "detrimental" stimulus-response behavior to spin out of control. What becomes amplified are the routines, all routines growing less to resemble initial responses and becoming somewhat self-contained, as in isolation, but not at all self-recursive. Not to mention the supply chain, which settles into its own "self-satisfied" routine that also moves further away from initial conditions while contributing and sustaining the corresponding "obesity helix". Qualifying as an epidemic, stimulus-response behavior merely reacts to both taste and options, and given that these options are mutually self-sustaining, this collaboration ultimately amplifies further from the normative "food and nutrition" routines of our initial "native" traits. It appears artificial in its modernist trappings, removed from primal and "natural" commands, and it is in that the subsequent amplification of the new learned routines are substantially removed from the initial "instinct" for nutrition. Such routines of reduplication, replication of patterns of behavior are amplifications that increase the volume and complexity, as well as removal, of original patterns and routines. Our (peculiarly American) socio-cultural epidemic of obesity merely reduplicates previous routines while amplifying the intensity of the information. Our fat now is not our fat then.

A great portion of our behavior descends from such amplification of and from primal routines: our living habits only resemble primal habits by description not in substance, as a rough frame of reference, but not in content. Integrity of the original is lost in the routine reduplication of information. We are as we were but what we were is not what we are. Our "spiraling" through successive amplified boosts take us further away, never returning to an "original" state, a state we can only refer to through copies we have made from previous copies.

Tracking other socio-cultural trends, fads, conventions, etc. The models of amplification and reduplication prove particularly applicable. Take period nostalgia, a construct of bottom-top complexity: the subroutine of individual nodes' sentimental reminiscent of "days gone by" converging into a mass socio-cultural "trend", resulting in imitations and copies of mementos and curios from the era. Our recent nostalgia for the 1970's was, of course, predictable. Of course, there was no actual return of the 70's; we somehow made room for the sweep of the arc of that nostalgia as the original was reduplicated from both memory and routine, resulting in an amplification of this information into a state of "mass nostalgia". This was, of course, made the more intense by the instantaneousness of our communication from the technology that had developed, a parallel routine that also developed, over time through reduplication and amplification. As it is, we will inevitably move away from this nostalgia as well, the arc descending as the sweep loses intensity, only to have it return in more diffused state, again barely recognizable as the nostalgia that preceded it.

Such tracking is often noticed but overlooked, especially as one is caught in the middle of the sweep; our perspective determines what we can perceive. We assume a shape of the whole from within the whole itself, much like we assume the shape of the Milky Way without actually having seen it from a perspective exterior and distant. Knowing both the amplification of the trend and its inevitable diminishment does not really aid our comprehension of events. Once amplification sets in, it is difficult to rein in the associated "hysteria" that allows it to build itself into a collective Weltanschauung, until it has exhausted itself. And it doesn't really "exhaust" itself as it "mutates' into another sweep, having become distant and removed from the original content. Even nostalgia itself, the nostalgia for nostalgia, obeys the same "law without law" of the helical sweep at the instigation of reduplication and amplification of information.

As we often neglect this turn of things, we also have among us operatives who find that the turn lends itself to their own machinations regarding the world. World political figures often seem (and I emphasize "seem to") manipulate elements for the advantage of their various agendas. And this is partially true, but more often than not merely "time" their efforts with the 'sweep' of the world.

Finally, closure! Or not….

So where loops serve as simple models to configure the interval of a relation between input and output, they cannot be extended any further. The notion that the loop is a self-contained, self-defining process is sufficient within the interval of the sweep itself, as feedback proves to be the operative and guiding principle.

But as it is, there is no continuous and self-same loop, given that each revolution adds/subtracts elements and in that absorption/repulsion action each revolution is distinguished as a difference in the feedback, the self-same is not returned. For example, each revolution differentiates itself in time as having been, as being, and as a becoming. And in each interval, some element or elements are absorbed, repelled, expelled, or altered. The alleged lock of the loop in the self-same, and there can be such a locking, fails to recognize the interval by which it transfers, or is amplified, into the next loop.

The closest approximation, by analogy or allegory, might be better demonstrated through the analogue tape loop (as was the function of the Echoplex machine): one removes the erase head and the tape, in the record mode, simultaneously plays the recorded information/sound and records a recording of the information/sound just played. Having removed the erased head, the player/recorder does not erase the previous information but layers it into multiple copies. Amplification of such sentient information does not always lead to clarification, and not all information is carried forward with sufficient clarity.

Take even the feedback of amplified guitars: the pickup on the guitar picks up the signal emanating from the amp and in turn sends it back to the amp and this continues until the amp reaches a threshold where it can no longer expand upon the signal but only sustains a saturated level of sound. But it did not arrive there as a self-same loop: the self-recognition of the feedback is arrived at through intervals of successive sweeps, notched up through differentiated signals.

Where, then, we assume a loop that regulates itself into the self-same, we are primarily dealing with a helical sweep that manages successive stages of amplified reduplication, arriving at a general stability through saturation that is only contained by the minimization of vibration and/or entropic contingencies. Theoretically it could go on forever, but it doesn't because it exhausts the amplitudes that sustained the sweep. We are then left with a simultaneous, layered superimposition of information that is both energetic and exhausted, same but different simultaneously. The difference in time and space, in character and content, is gained through only the slightest removal from the "original" and the subsequent loss of integrity, whether through depletion or augmentation. Each "sweep" is primarily a copy of the previous sweep, it is not the same, nor is it different, but is a copy of a copy…. Amplification is achieved merely by the action and resonance of the output's return as a copy. And, again, the action is indifferent to details in that it does not "care" for what is or what is not "valuable", it selects without discrimination or only from what is most pronounced. Selectivity according to some criteria of value is nonexistent in the sweep of reduplication, and amplifies whatever is persistent, present, or pronounced.

Loops, sweeps, and spirals are not the way of the world and are not necessarily found in nature. As it is, it all obeys more of an anthropic principle that it wouldn't exist if it were not for the existence of humans. It is the result of how humans experience the world and their own consciousness, how humans experience the world through how the mechanism of human consciousness processes time, space, and objects.

The name of Schrödinger's Cat is Felix

"The global instant 'now' is defined to be all of those events contained in the leaf of the constant mean curvature foliation which passes through the Earth at the present time."
-Pg. 660 The Anthropic Cosmological Principle, John D. Barrow and Frank J. Tipler

Here: stained glass. Or mosaics. Bits and pieces put together to make up a whole. So what does this all mean then? Do we perceive things as distinct, discrete incidents, or distinctions in the incident of their occurring? We look at stained glass and recognize the figure the pattern suggests. But no part of the glass, by itself, suggests the overriding figure.

Maybe then, on the other hand, what we perceive isn't as 'selective' or incidental as we have come to believe, that is, we are not "seeing" one thing at a time, but everything at once. And if it wasn't for this everything at once we wouldn't, or couldn't, see at all.

How often do we mistake something distant for something close? How often do we confuse the dimensions of something distant for the actual dimensions? Visual jokes abound about scale, how something distant is gauged to be extremely small but on approach is revealed to be something very large.

I had that encounter on my first visit to Colorado. An acquaintance and myself were driving about on a reconnaissance of the area for potential sites for a performance event. I kept telling her to "drive over to that peak", seeing these wondrous peaks and mountains as discrete points in the terrain. She countered with, and I paraphrase, "Well, they look different from a distance. You drive over there, it will disappear." The approach to peaks and hills are more often gradual. The "wonder" would cease. On closer examination, it would no longer be a mountain, but a slope.

Illusions don't exist in the world, a priori. They are not "out there" for us to discover. We enable and encounter them all the time. It is the inherent flaws and shortcomings as well as our strengths and advantages of our cognitive and perceptual mechanisms. They might prove problematic but often enough don't.

We benefit from mistakes, errors and flaws. Not every copy or the copy we copy from is flawed, or even "perfect". But our insistence that some sort of conclusive judgment classify these events in categories of valued and unvalued seem unreasonably tainted, burdening the already overburdened, taxed cognitive system with speculative guarantees of truth and profundity. That such "abstractions" ought be the precondition of the truth of what is sensed is a formality, yet another condition of a long history of the tradition of a convention, a habit.

Point of fact, consciousness is limited to what and how it can process. There is a general homogenization of perceived information, a reduction of specific, and multiple details to generalized patterns. It is not only a matter of training or learning, there is a requirement of cognitive processing that it can only assume from what it can sense, a myopia that descends from the primal and initial conditions, one would suppose. One mind cannot process more that what is evident, so the generalities must suffice.

To look at every detail, to inventory and process every element on its own merits precipitates a collapse into a morass of interrelated and contingent details, all of which most cognitive apparatuses would falter.

Most of us see the world as 2-d panel with 3-d appointments, or process it as so. And that is due to the shortcomings of our neural-sensory mechanisms. But it is the habit of registering and accepting conclusions drawn from the perceptions accomplished by the sensorial apparatus that becomes and informs our traditions and conventions. Proof from sense alone does not automatically lead to the truth of anything, especially sense, but we have based so much of our ideological and philosophical conclusions on this premise for so long that it proves difficult to extricate ourselves from this.

Dissemble the mosaic and you are left with small bits of polished stone but no mosaic. You've sacrificed the unity of the presentation for the disunity of the ensemble of unrelated particles, the various and self-sufficient elements. Seeing the whole should not admit to some privilege of the whole over the parts, but somehow it does through social convention, context, or contingency. Film has its own disproportions: the "illusion" of movement is achieved not merely by the projection of the chain of framed images at 24 frames per second but of our retinal/neural retention of images, persistence of vision. An image "impresses" just long enough to construct continuity. Cultures unaccustomed to 24 fps (and there are fewer and fewer) cannot perceive movement in film, could not follow a movie. Is this a flaw in their cognition? Or ours (speaking in terms of Euro-centric placement)? It was often thought it was theirs.

The delicacy of part/whole dynamics is only betrayed by the shift in perspective; we see a whole from one angle, we see parts from another. How we've come to allow certain favoritism reveals not a standard truth in the dichotomy but a flaw in our collective cognition, a myopias regarding substance and event. As ancient survival machines, we cannot afford to be too perceptive. We needed to see wholes; we needed to see the forest and not the trees. Our survival depends upon it, even as the conditions for survival have relaxed. But perceiving substance where there is none does not verify truth. There is the fact of there being something there, but the truth is that what is there is more an ensemble of elements and forces.

Take light for example. We see light as if external to ourselves, as if something generated from a point of origin distant from ourselves. The transitory event of our material being must also look away from the light that permeates it. Not some "spiritual" light that illuminates us as some sort of Coleman Lantern, the phantom of the Self lit by the soul, but by the light generated by every particle tenuously bound in the aggregate of our being.

By having observed the passage of time we have observed the event of light. In having been, we have been light. Materiality is not illuminated by light but generates light in order to illuminate itself.

Some have postulated that we are the eyes of the universe, the medium by which the universe acknowledges itself. But in that light does not describe its own history, it neither ends nor begins. If there is one conception of history (that is not related to time per se, but only as that catalogue of being and having been) that we would have difficulty comprehending, it is the one that describes history as being bent. As we know that light and time can be bent through gravitational force, can we accept such pliability for history? Possibly only as it is also light.

Causality is something of an error. Are beginnings caused? Are causes beginnings? Can we trace causes to beginnings? Beginnings are arbitrarily designated increments of convenience, ways we package time into events that we can reference or recall. A habit of human cognition, we simply categorize attributes into recognizable points of reference: names, images, concepts. This referential taxonomy, a taxonomy that has little to do with categorization even as it categorizes, given that the elements are unrelated and disparate, conceals the fact that nothing really holds the world together, that this disparity suggests the insecurity of matter, place, and principles.

Is there a beginning to history? A cause?

The world is barely there, barely composed, barely whole. What keeps it together, say, gravitational pull, is itself contingent on there being mass. The mutual pull of matter is tenuous: all could just as easily fall away as it does come together. The incidence of our being whole and together is (co-) incidental to the "natural" condition of imminent dispersion.

Our (false) sense of security, supported by the bundled flaws in our programming, allows for only minute levels of awareness regarding patterns of light and matter. We must assume solidity if only out of need or necessity as directed by our instinct for survival. To see our selves as matter perforated by light would directly confront the carefully constructed architecture we have made of ourselves.

Our history must then also appear to us as a solid line of progress, a point A to point B narrative clock of events and figures. Given the difficulties that non-linearity presents to conventional human cognition, it is easier for us to arrive at "facts" through, arguably, direct paths of conjecture and comparative analysis: what is true for us must also be true for history.

Even if we knew of a beginning, we could not, with any certainty, establish it as a cause. We barely know where we begin and the world ends. Separated from the world by a thin, porous sheath composed of a temporary collaboration of molecules whose atomic structure is itself at odds with the neighboring atomic structures as well as itself, we assume interiority where there is none. And from this phantom interiority we assume wholeness and continuity, despite the fact that we could just as easily break apart, atomize, dematerialize.

The parts are greater than the whole, as the whole must contend with the precipice of its imminent collapse.

Yet, even as we know of this, as persons who could just as easily become unbound and dissipate, we are better off for believing ourselves and the world as whole. Having the psychic buffer of our being we can approach the world and negotiate it.

And from this, we must also assume a cause for ourselves. Naturally, then, we infer a cause for the world. "If I am here, I started some place. If I started some place, then so has the world". Our ancient lines of association, the faulty inference of causes and effects, place us in positions of magical, primal thought patterns. From the assumption of cause we infer the appearance of a beginning.

Our glimpse into the precarious hold of matter has not resulted in any substantial change in our approach to life. Now, why is that? This is not an attestation as to the truth of our medieval patterns of thought, only as to its staying power, its tenacity. We cannot give up the phantom of our ghosts because we are so attached to the idea; our primitive notion of soul lends us comfort, a coping mechanism, a point of reference that affords us an ease of negotiation through the world and our relations to others.

Seeing, then, our selves and our world as permeable, porous, would not, in the medieval structure we operate within, benefit us. It would work in another system, a system appropriate to it, but no such system exists. And without a doubt, given how difficult it is to shed ourselves of our medieval inclinations, we would certainly turn to the practice of worship and ritual to confirm our "new" approach.

That would certainly indicate a beginning that we would be witness to. But could we? The progression of events leading up to a beginning fails to indicate the characteristics. Parameters are suggested but inconclusive. From what point is arbitrarily designated as to be a beginning we forget the factors leading up to and exceeding this point.

This shifting continuum of apparently discrete increments can only be enabled through the usual assumptions of wholeness. Being incapable of comprehending time as less than discrete and corporal, our limitations dictate that time is as substantial as space.

The problem is that the instance of our position in space and time, and our comprehension thereof (or lack thereof) conceals the infinity of the multiple within the finitude of our existence. Being that things are now present even as they are transitional, held together through the force of mass and the event of their being, extension in time is not proof of infinity beyond the point at which the world and we "are".

It isn't that the world is lacking in material, it is abundant to the point of absurdity. And in whatever fashion consciousness must assemble a notion of completeness from the evidence provided by the senses, we are incorrigible regarding the requirement that things must be inviolable, solid, and in place.

Where a topographic map of, say, the Grand Canyon accounts for the surface features of the assembled geology, a true map, as incommensurable as it would be, would account for every grain of sand, flow of water, of light, and incidences of erosion. It would indicate the cascade of the simultaneous noise of particles falling into place and apart from it. Of course no map would be relevant at any time as it would be specific, whereas a general map would. Here, the map is the territory. Or I should say, it is *simultaneously* a map of *a* territory and *the* territory itself.

The immediacy of our information environment has somehow entitled us to assume history where there is none. Is it because of this accelerated immediacy of information and the fleeting, transitory nature of it that we seek to embrace any instant as an event with "historic consequences'?

Our own lives are "histories", but not historic, but histories nonetheless. Like art, the surplus of histories threatens to undermine the import of the term. Designating an event as "historic" has relevance only as to how it alters our relationship to things, to the world, to our selves. And if time is without end, then it is, much like the light that fails to acknowledge a source, as not having begun.

To assume that any history, either collectively or individually, is sacrosanct, inviolable and precise in its composition, neglects the floating and pooling of wild and disparate elements that neither obey laws of linear progression nor rules of conduct that inspire queues and family lineages. As the genealogy of time itself is inextricably bound with that of light, our history floats away from us, only to return as degraded as the image of Felix the Cat [7] that began the new information epoch.

The point about history that people forget is how oblivious history is to itself.

---

[7] RCA's first experimental television transmissions began in 1928 by station W2XBS (New York-Channel #1) in Van Cortlandt Park and then moved to the New Amsterdam Theater Building, transmitting 60 line pictures. The 13" Felix the Cat figure made of paper mâche was placed on a record player turntable and was broadcast using a mechanical scanning disk to an electronic kinescope receiver. (http://felixthecat.com/history.html) Is it a matter of time till the earth passes through this initial transmission again?

History is not itself historic. Neither is it a continuum of fluid, linear progression. To describe it as composed of discrete parcels of events is also problematic in that this assumes definition of beginning and end where there is none. What we think about history, how we describe it, is contingent on the perspective from which we view it. And because there is such an abundance of history, of histories, histories that defy time, histories that are contingent on the habits of human cognition, one could say the history of human cognition, the case for fluid passage, of singular flow, is tenuous. What we have are histories that, like light, are themselves multiple particulates sliding into and over each other, forming into patterns that appear discrete from one perspective, continuous from other perspectives but have no relation to history in general nor to themselves or each other. Our multiple histories that would not exist if it were not for our consciousness of them are there only by virtue of having been observed. And in having been observed they have been "altered", disturbed, and, subsequently, "violable."

Regarding the analogy to light, the pattern formed of photons pushing against each other; can a case be made for the inverse? If there are many and different histories, are there many and different forms of light? Or is light pretty much the same from one source to another? And even then, is it the same light?[8]

---

[8] Recall Heraclitus here, as in fragment #81: "Just as the river where I step is not the same, and is, so I am as I am not." (*Fragments: The Collected Wisdom of Heraclitus*, Translated by Brooks Haxton, 2001 Viking Penguin.)

And this is the problem I am having explaining myself: we process things as generalizations; whereas it is quite possible they exist as an amalgamation of superimpositions, the superposition, of elements and events. We anticipate substance and solidity but process the incident of (or coincident of) disparate energies and dissembled particles. A street is processed as a whole, we perceive and comprehend wholeness, solidity, but given the shortcomings of our cognitive apparatus, we cannot (or should not) perceive the dynamic of various levels of particles and elements. The final event, even as it is a composite of sub-events, patterns, and the action superposition of subsystems, is all that we can process.

Is this all, then, a cosmic ruse? A joke? No such punch line here: all this reveals is how deeply primitive we are, how we are removed from our primal being only by degrees, not in kind. There is coincidence of things, as accident, and coincidence as concurrence, simultaneity.

Think, I suppose, of one of those anatomical graphics, common to old encyclopedias and medical dictionaries, where sheaths of transparencies are laid atop of each other. On the first level we see the whole, the body of the body. As we turn back one sheath, removing the first layer, we see the body at another level of interiority, maybe the cardio-pulmonary system, and the dermis, whatever. One peels back each layer, dislocating the whole of the body. One returns the layer and we perceive wholeness.

And it is this "final event" that we process, and it is this that we copy and reduplicate in our cognitive systems. You see each portion of the world as a whole because you process it as such. It is the limit of our cognitive apparatus because it is all that is demanded of it.

And this is fine for survival, a routine of simplification that smoothes and homogenizes perceptible observables into recognizable patterns, a routine that is simultaneously confirmed, reinforced, denied and corrected through our interactions with others. The routine of simplification is both a product of shortcomings in the cognitive apparatus and the context and conventions of our social circumstances.

If a tree falls in the forest and no one is there, no, it doesn't make a sound. But even if we are there, it doesn't engender sound of its own but initiates a process of superimposed events that make sound possible. In the micro-units of aural phenomenon, we could discern discrete packages of a sound-producing events whose reliance on neighboring packages results in an ensemble of events that make the "sound" of this tree possible. We "stack" up these events, generalize them and process them as "wholes", disposing of the discrete for the continuum.

Does any of this indicate the existence of a material reality outside of consciousness? We certainly have our debates, particularly in quantum physics, between the camps of Einstein and Bohr. 'Knowing' certainly does not confirm such, nor does sense. We can certainly acknowledge that there is indeed material reality; we simply lack any definitive affirmation. We have evidence, we share evidence, but ultimately all we are left with is an assumption.

On one hand, we are not so removed from the world that we are left in isolated tanks dreaming of our quotidian lives, a la the move "The Matrix". Yet on the other hand, we are not so immersed in the world that we can ascertain and participate in an unmediated experience of reality. We are not protected; we are simply not developed. Between our selves (even as it "is us") and the world is this sheath of skin and the sensory array that informs us. From this we assemble our knowledge of the world (and simultaneously, our selves), a knowledge that is never direct, never unmediated, but translated and represented. That is: the body experiences the world as the body interprets the world. Our cognition is then directed not by direct experience but replicated and reduplicated patterns. It would be, then, this play of reduplication again, this copying of copies. This having bearing only on how we cognize, how we process and transmit information.

And this returns us to this problem of skin. In no way should one surmise from the material fact of skin that this sensory array demarcates a distinction of interiority and exteriority. The self that skin "informs' remains the skin itself. In probably yet another tenuous analogy, it would be like "thinking glass", a surface of neural points that only informs the circuitry of the skin. Metzinger proposes the self to be transparent: something seen through and seen with. As it is, this array of sensory components, the ensemble of neural networks, it conceals "nothing", it encloses "nothing", particularly the "phantasm" of soul. It is the mosaic that we see and that we are simultaneously. This mosaic of experience and events that construct a recognizable and reduplicatable pattern, a mosaic that, if the various tesserae were subtracted, nothing would remain but the particles and elements the mosaic was constructed from. There would be no ghost, no soul, and no phantom of our being.

What we return to is this lived fact of organic completion and this less directly observable fact of incompletion. We perceive and sense the all-at-once of lived completion, we process it as completion and continuity, which, at this level, might as well be complete even as it is the simultaneity of parallel and distributed material. Is this as primitive as it might appear? An evolution by degrees from primal cognition, or the product of constraints that we can occasionally see past?

And probably neither, in that there is no option. It is merely the default process that we can simultaneously see past and cannot escape. We are both "primal" and "advanced" at the same time.

Culturally, through history, our improvements, our "peaks" of amplification have both aggravated and relieved our difficulties but cannot be shown to have created them. Whereas our improvements in science and culture, we are continually bothered by the retention of our "primal", oppositional tendencies. We live in this in-between of peaks of scientific/cultural progress and troughs of primal, irrational instincts, all overlapping and antagonistic. Are we equipped to deal with this? No and yes, and whether or not this is deemed fragmentation and we assume that fragmentation remains an antagonism, is problematic and contributive to social ills by the tint of the diabolical we attach to it, that would not be fair: fragmentation does exist and our minds are there to make sense of it, organize it, even if in doing so we contribute to it. Such is the nature of the mechanism. In that everything is mind, our models are there to answer for it and address it as such. Not doing so is what is detrimental. Not getting your bearings in the fragmented and indeterminism of the world, of both the mind and reality, of not coming to terms with the fragmentary nature of existence, is what thwarts and arrests human development. The assumption of a false unity is as equally detrimental to the human condition as the failure to correctly calculate our position in the fragmentary. Should we distinguish between culture and nature? Are these things that definite? Can we draw such distinctions? If culture is a biologically determined, a product of biological processes, extending from thought and sensation, then no such distinction can be made. Culture is not "natural" but it is nature. What happens for culture and our observation of it goes also for nature. These distinctions must be tossed out: the notion that the boundaries between our knowing and the world are decisive, definite and determined; they are, instead, pliable and permeable. We indeed exist in the overlap between many elements, that if we envision ourselves as spheres with influence, mine and yours and the world co-exist, superimposed over each other.

What must be contended with is the very simultaneity of all-at-once that makes life and cognition even possible. Or maybe: can it be, should it be, contended with? See, nothing of the world indicates a viable contentiousness; learning to be puts us in a contentious, adversarial relationship that only results from our native inability to process what is seemingly unobservable or assumed to be inessential.

Even here I am guilty of an inconsistency, and I would have to admit it is probably attributable to my own cognitive deficiencies, inherited I suppose, a tradition an indoctrination that is difficult to extricate oneself from. Where I am asserting that there is no distinction of internal/external mechanics to be drawn in the human organism, there is still this matter of skin that seemingly (seemingly!) makes that distinction for us. And there is still this looming possibility that nothing exists outside of our sensorial array and our processing of information.

This distinction is there because it rises out of the fundamental and simplest of conclusions to be drawn from the information available to us. And not information per se, but information as processed by the organism. We assume differentiation and distinction because of the limits of our flesh-based senses. And yes, the distinction is there: interims of material existence as one is, objects are as they are, but our processing arrives at a conclusion that draws a broader distinction than what is there or necessary, establishing greater distinctions such as soul and individuality that drives material being into permutations of idealism and spiritualism, both the result of a feudalism of hosted being and privilege.

But this is not necessarily so. Basing all of our cultural, social, and ideological privilege on this non-existent privilege of being, of being cognitive, negates our associations with materiality. Such negation leads us further away from truth, or should I say a more effective and realistic relation to the Universe.

The distinction that we can make is merely one of place, position in space. Even as the cognitive flaws that issue from our fatal misinterpretation of information gathered through the flesh-born senses might assume, as the amplified sweep of cognitive feedback and feed forward from reduplicated initial conditions contributes to it, we can still ascertain what is us, what is out there, and what this "is" might be composed of without sacrificing spatial individualization. Our cognitive flaws should not lead us to believe that nothing exists, but, again, it does point to the fact that we don't really know with any certainty. Our own materiality interferes with our comprehension of material reality itself. Everything is echoes, echoes on sonar, static, noise, an all-at-once that we process into forms and shapes, forms and shapes distinguished from the noise that is our world. In the noise of the all-at-once we can "see" what we want, what we need, and what we can assume is there.

As it is, we don't really "sort it all out", and in some ways it is all sorted out for us; intermittent bursts of organization are inevitable and with such frequent, rapid succession that we assume continuity as the memory persists. But this noise of the world, this refraction of the world, produces/produced perceived seeming wholes and fissures, disjoints and completions where there is none, or might be the opposite. We perceive "wholes" where there are only refractions of multiple and simultaneous parts, particles, fissures, fractures, layers, waves and holes.

Refraction is everywhere, sensorial and tutorial, ideological and cultural, physical and cognitive. From these refractions we must synchronize information into cognizable instances. And refraction, multiple and simultaneous, obviously can be deceptive, unless one comprehends the laws: "**Refraction** is the change in direction of a wave due to a change in its speed. This is most commonly observed when a wave passes from one medium to another at an angle. Refraction of light is the most commonly observed phenomenon, but any type of wave can refract when it interacts with a medium, for example when sound waves pass from one medium into another or when water waves move into water of a different depth." We see the straw in a glass of water as fractured, but it is not. Yet to assume that it is to assume from facts that are not in evidence but as assumed.

Or are they? I mean, it is evident, and therefore factual as long as one observes. Once you tamper with the evidence, then one realizes that the straw is indeed whole. Does water "break" things? Obviously, the observer affects the object. And to arrive at the "truth" of the situation, one must interfere. And, yet, the "truth" of the new event is also the event of fact that attracts a density, a concatenation of other and different events.

But we can extend this into our cognitive model's spatio-temporal experience of the world, as lived present in nature and culture, the sphere of reduplication that is contingent on memory. And in and of itself in the all-at-once, all of these events we dichotomize into distinct patterns, superimpose themselves; culture/nature simultaneity results in yet other refractions that can confuse and obfuscate "facts" while concealing the very fact of refraction, not to mention the refraction active in the apparatus of cognition itself.

Along all these simultaneous fields of discrete components, passing in and out of perception, relations and associations are either discovered or fabricated. There is material substance here, nothing is so much an idealism as to not be tangible to some degree, observed in some manner, but the demand placed on cognition begs simplicity and shortcuts, especially given the rote survivalism that persists in our specie's neurology.

Throughout all this I am pretty aware that I've managed to associate and propose a number of problematic, if not self-negating, components. So it probably would be time to explore these and how they relate to this odd little theory.

For one thing, the emphasis on the "discrete". If there is nothing but the "all-at-once", a notion that implies continuity, how could there be "discrete elements"? How could things register as discrete events?

For one thing, it is necessary to put aside the conventional valorization of individuality. The discrete I am employing here does not emphasize a premise of individuality, autonomy of part over whole. Discrete merely references the instant, the spatio-temporal event of matter and aggregates thereof. I understand it this way, as each event is the concatenation of multiple and distinct events and instances, discernible on the level of their coming into existence, of being present, then even the seemingly singular and continuous event is composed of multiple and discrete events.

And we would also have to view this "coming into being" as itself an event, even to the level of the microscopic, These "fields" of particle-events appear continuous in the rough generalization, but closer observation establishes further distinctions. Ensembles, then, of such distinctions result in intermittent temporal events, their "passing" in and out of perception, an orchestration (without intent of purpose, without awareness of adjacent events) of phenomenal unity that is contingent on its being observed.

This inevitably leads us into the notion of infinity. Amongst the many "misreadings" we possess, one of the most persistent is to associate "infinity" with "eternity", "infinity" with "endless space". We assume an open-ended time scale as well as a crowding of finite material objects existing in an infinite space of open-ended confinement. Whether or not it is "true" is beside the point, in fact it is sufficient: pragmatically we need not really concern ourselves with it. Infinity is irrelevant, at least infinity as it is space and time extended without limit. But I would propose here that infinity is not understandable as a past-present-future construction, but only as it exists only as of the present. And here would be the key to the all-at-once, the infinite simultaneity of everything as everything is present.

Infinity, which is to say, by virtue of being infinite, already doesn't exist. That is, outside of the strictly mathematical or the inferential construct, it is neither a fact of space nor a characteristic of time. Indeed there is an "infinity" of infinities, only as they remain discrete packets of vertically extended increments, positioned in the transitional now. Time only exists as it is present, not as it has passed. And the things that compose time, the things that inhabit it, both objects and abstractions, only truly exist, as they are present for that miniscule nanosecond that they are present.

Recognizing and situating ourselves in that increment we refer to as Now, even as it is immediately transitional, is both something advantageous and yet strikingly difficult. (The gauze of the Zen-like apprehension of "Being in the Now" does not suffice, in that it, the Now, is always a having-been, not a being. It is sufficient for *comfortably* comprehending being and becoming, but not *accurate*, nor even very compelling).

The assumed loop of cyclic time is a misinterpretation. Time is not a quality, it is a quantity. Time is not cyclical even as it is the circulation of things and events. Here is a primary limitation of variation in these constructs, circulations, and their organizations, a limited (although limitless) number of elements. It is this limitation that we experience as cyclical.

We could not process time as discrete events: it would be overwhelming, impossible. But time is such: discrete but violable "packets" that rise and pass, arise and deplete. We process time as continuum but it exists in discrete events. It is not noticed because the events, the multiple systems and subsystems, while simultaneous are not synchronous, they "move" parallel and simultaneous at different and various rates. So the discrete events are not noticed: given that we can only observe one at a time, or everything at once, we assume continuity. The unique flaw that bends perception…like flaws in jewelry…. this is what is "unique" to each individual. We own our flaw and it marks every perception. At its most basic, the mind relies upon a platform of loops, reduplications, and input-only openness. This primal loop orientation makes it difficult to comprehend discrete systems, especially time, so we assume looping because that's how our primitive neurology processes things and perceived events. We are bi-polar in that sense: conscious and cognizant (parallel) and yet basic and primitive (linear). It might exist "in here" but does not necessarily exist "out there".

Yet, the all-at-once is not the convergence of the infinite, at least as it is cognized. We cannot assume an infinite from what is before us, only as we can comprehend it is an extension of the immediate and observable into the unobservable and gradient. What cannot be seen can only be speculated or at least approximated. The all-at-once of material immediacy subject to refraction through superimposition and superposition, assumes dimensional dynamics that trace and retrace, copy and re-copy, arcs and trajectories of material information. This includes thought; there is no reason to subtract or distinguish thought from materiality, based only upon its supposed "abstraction". Tactility is about the only criteria employed to distinguish abstract from concrete, strangely enough leading to yet the "misreading" and valorization of tactility as proof of being. But as "proof of truth" it is insufficient, given the limitations of the sensory array. Skin doesn't lie, it confirms, but even then the information gained from it, translated and processed, is mediated. Such truth is not immediate.

Rushing about us, then, are multi-layered trajectories that, through refraction and superimposition, construct transitional instances that are cognized as complete events in themselves. The appearance of a unified and continuous world is attributable to the shorthand that human cognition subjects information to. Now, this is not to say, again, that there isn't a world "out there". There is, but it is, to us, only as it is mediated by our cognitive processes and disturbed by our having observed it.

Assume this fragmentary condition as something of a puzzle, each piece by itself essential to the composition overall, but by itself essential only to itself (and even in being singular remains self-contextualized). Our problem isn't with the fragmentary condition but how we interpret it, how the brain processes it. Why should or do we react in kind to the fragmentary? Because we do not understand the fragmentary and insist on a unity where there is none, engendering further fragmentation….

Refraction is the result of the self- or auto-composition of the world, even in the initial state prior to its being cognized or comprehended; the various and discrete elements "mounting up", in discrete transitional events, into the sum of the experienced. A phenomenal thing must either pass through the multiple layers and subsequently refract in their presence or must be created from them, from the interstices of element vectors converging upon each other. What is only as it is assembled from available elements.

This, the all-at-once, is less a problem for perception but more for cognition, in that objects at the entry level of sensorial input, assuming a Kantian distinction of the noumenal, are processed with a lesser degree of difficulty. It is the cognition of the phenomenal that things get more complex. This, of course, is not readily available to us but is accessible through thought, through thinking-through the superimposed. But even in this, nothing is immediately available. Think in terms of pixilation, either the pointillism of Seurat, or analog color television (this does beg yet another allegory with technology which is always antecedent to human cognition. But then do we invent to explain and define or do we define by invention? Would it be inappropriate to assume that technological innovations have a hidden, semantic function? A language of explanation by example?) Points laid out in space, whether attributable to physical space or mental space, are sufficient, even inviolable as things-in-themselves but gain a velocity of purpose through their relationship with other points. And in that these ensembles of phenomenal points gather force in numbers, in a certain noise of differentiation, events construct themselves through reflection, refraction, and superimposition, that point to an evolving and escalating complexity of cognitive events. Given that complexity, stemming from the positive feedback with intermittent limit states of cognitive reduplication, our primitive cognitive apparatus must process things by simplifying the information into easily processable contexts. "Simplifying" may be too simple a designation; smoothing, rounding off or down, quantifying may be more accurate, but such abridgement also makes the system vulnerable to misinterpretations and mistakes.

In, then, the all-at-once that we are immersed in, we create, interpret and map as elements and events mount up, leading to both revelation, in the context of cognitive abilities that are advanced and less affected by interference, and mistakes, in the context of less developed cognitive abilities and running greater degrees of interference.

Assuming, then, a vertical stratification of elements in the interstice of the phenomenal and transitional "now", we arrive at infinity only as it is a verticality and not horizontal. In this regard, the infinite remains only as it is experienced transitionally, that is, infinity is only as it is finitely known. The infinite all-at-once of the "now" passes instantaneously into the finitude of the having-been.

So where we assume we can comprehend the interstice of the all-at-once of infinity as that which spreads before and after this present, the array of entities throughout the universe in time and space, this isn't necessarily so. The infinite is certainly not confined to the vast of everything before us, but is truly known in the present, as it is the infinity of increments in the measure of the present.

The temporal finitude of infinity: infinity does not exist in time. That is: it does not extend into the future nor into the past (the SEEMINGLY infinite of the past of things are still a limited, finite set) …it does not extend on a horizontal axis of past-present-future but only occurs on the vertical of the present, extending only as it is manifested in the now. Is there infinity of nows? No, not as they exist but only as they have existed in memory.

It is in memory that we locate the "trick" of continuity, the persistence of events in the mind, a persistence that allows for the perception of "forward" progression, or, at least, movement. This despite the fact that the faculty of memory is entirely reliant on reduplication processes. We never remember an event, an object, an idea; we reduplicate the memory as a copy from a copy.

Much like visual persistence that makes movement possible in film, we have persistence of cognition, or cognitive persistence, that makes continuity possible. Continuity is entirely anthropic, contingent on the presence and position of an observer, an observer that must account for him/her self in the world and his/her relation to the world. Continuity is only possible through there being an observer present and the faculty of cognitive persistence.

We observe the passing of the all-at-once in nano-seconds. Cognition, it would seem, would be "timed" to view progression of events as a consistent and continuous trajectory. Where as film is projected at something like 24 frames per second, we process the eventual far faster.

Memory, of course, aids and abets persistence, as it is the seat of persistence. Even as memory may be "filed" in a decomposed condition, as it is a copy of a copy with a corresponding loss of structural integrity (or phenomenal integrity) it is the impress of memory that allows for chronological persistence, eluding the all-at-once and assuming past-present-future temporal architecture. For us, something must exist in the past and memory tells us this is so. What memory doesn't admit is that nothing exists in the past in that the past is no longer. All that is required is what is present; memory exists only as it benefits the observer, not time itself (but given the dynamics of observer/object-world dynamics, time benefits in being observed).

Persistence, cognitive persistence informed by memory, homogenizes events into a spatio-temporal continuum. Our assumptions of cycles and returns, repetition and regulatory negative feedback, stems from our reliance on mnemonic persistence; we coordinate our existence with the points that memory provides. That our condition of persistence functions as negative feedback system runs parallel to our condition of the positive feedback system, with intermittent limit states, of our cognitive development. Ideas start at the ground zero of perception, but quickly escalate through progressive reduplication out of control, into a "dizzying" noise. That these two contrary conditions would run parallel often results in some dissonance, some significant ruptures in one's comprehension even as it provides significant development in cognitive abilities of persons and social systems.

Memory regulates even as the memory pattern loses integrity. The copy-of-a-copy that is the memory still provides coordinates for a person's self-construct as well as the social-construct. Time seems as one piece, even as we recognize its exhaustion, the demise of the transitional all-at-once of infinity. Time could then only be memory, but that would be between you and me, the community and myself. It is our pact, our consensus that time exists as it is experienced, but as this is coerced through the dissemination of representations of events, we all assume the same memory.

Remembering is different than memory. Remembering is forced; it is intentional retrieval of information, a retrieval abetted by reduplication. We assume we are remembering directly but are reduplicating from reduplicated information removed from a source. Memory is information derived from the fluctuation of saccades of consciousness, it is neither source nor copy but that blind and distributed bank of "stored" information. In memory, nothing is distinguished by item, but only as it is recalled. When memory becomes remembered, we assemble categories that respond and coordinate them into accessible, reduplicated nodes. Memory is the incoherent pool of dissimilar information, remembering is the ensemble of memory assembled.

Remembering is employed to provide continuity as the now-point of the infinite all-at-once departs. We don't battle with memories for accuracy, we battle with remembering, looking for accuracy, as it is the coordinates of the continuity of our identity construct. These shifting, modular and transparent components of episodic memory superimpose themselves over present cognition, causing a temporal refraction of past and present events as remembered and as encountered. Episodic memory is inherently refractive as it is reduplicative: no single memory is itself the "original"; every recall is a reduplication of an adjacent memory. Memory is not, despite our attendance to it, replicative, it is entirely reduplicative. Memory replicates nothing, but we do reduplicate from stored information, assembling from connections and refractions a "view" of the past. Yet we assume a correspondence with truth, that to have remembered is sufficient evidence of truth of event remembered. These transparent "panels" also join the all-at-once, further confounding the processing of information as we volunteer yet another layer of elements into the all-at-once of the present.

Memory/remembering in itself, as it is working memory, is not problematic; it is essential to learning, processing, and employing information. What does become problematic is the construct of past-time we call "memories", episodic memory, those directed re-stagings of past events as tangible evidence of having been. Assembling and re-assembling points of information that flag past events, we re-visit past times that ought to have been forgotten but now linger as the residual re-enactment of past-time, thus nostalgia and temporal continuity. Reinforced by episodic memory, the self-construct establishes temporal coordinates of past and present that provide continuity; and continuity is the assurance that in having been, one is being now and will become tomorrow.

The thing is, episodic memory, through our native penchant to confuse and misinterpret information with evidence when it is only information, seemingly contrives to deceive us (be aware there that the appearance of intention to contrive and intended deception is also a result of misinterpretation) by allowing us to assume a lasting permanence of past and passing events. And socially, we have extended the life of episodes by mutually encouraging its lasting value, by placing an incredible, and inflationary, value on memories themselves, no longer seeing them as teaching moments for working memory but living events for episodic. How we've gotten that way, through the positive feedback of social reduplication effects, I'll save for a corresponding chapter.

But for now, I would venture to say we don't forget enough. The current insistence that we "remember everything" is antithetical to the "true" nature of time and event. This dysfunction is common to everyone, though, a routine condition, because A) the body interferes with knowledge of the world, in that it mediates information, and B) the body sometimes "gets it wrong", in that it interprets. And even then, the body knows this about itself, or at least we can come to know this through our cognitive faculties, but would just as well forget.

Not every event expires with the passing of the all-at-once. Times may vary. Durations are variable on the horizontal stratification of simultaneous events. Some events on various scales will be of a "longer" or shorter duration given scale or intensity. So, what we might not be witness to is the simultaneous exhaustion of everything, the immediate extinction of events in time, but lengths and residual retention. Everything occurs all at once, but not everything is immediate depleted in their passing and are certainly not reliant on the neighboring components or even on the architecture of the all-at-once.

There is, in this massive, monstrous all-at-once differentials in the stratifications of events that occupy the transitional Now where residual, delayed duration of events increase complexity and thus refraction. And refraction is the effect that is most prominent here, that emerges from this complexity. Perception and cognition "passing through" at this point, or events/things passing through as being observed must pass through this complexity, but do not do so unscathed: they are refracted in the multitude of stratifications. So, what is observed is not entirely what was original in its departure. In fact, as refraction is so prevalent, much of what we see is not really itself but merely the sum of refraction. It might be a straw in the glass, but it is a broken straw that we observe.

Refraction then is the mark of cognitive processing and there is no way that anything observed or perceived can be guaranteed to remain sufficiently whole or unaffected.

It is this refraction and the emergent noise that accompanies it that constitutes the world we are conscious of, a consciousness that does not process directly but through reduplicated packets of information filed in our neural network, and it is this, the refractions, the noise, the reduplications that constitute the world as we CAN know it,

I would even postulate that the self is itself the product of multiple refraction, noise, and reduplication.

"…time may arise from the way that the universe is partitioned; what we perceive as time reflects the relations among its pieces." (Scientific American, pg. 59, June 2010). It is this, the multiple and various partitions, that bounce, reflect, and refract their information off all of these pieces that are observed and even then the observation is itself bounced, reflected, refract and reduplicated. It is the observed, the observer, and the observation that is refracted in the multiple partitions.

Our notion of time itself is plagued with variables and conjectures, most of which are overrun with artificial partitions, partitions constructed from social convention and mnemonic habits. The persistence of memory, as it is spread and distributed not only through the transitional increments of experienced Now, but as these memories, reduplicated throughout transitional points, must also be accounted in the all-at-once, even if not evidential and concrete. Such persistence subverts the procession of time through an ensemble of multiple "time keepers" into the stall of time in a singular time command. We organize time into a singular uniformity even as the all-at-once suggest otherwise, that memory-based time is not a reliable timekeeper but given its persistence, it furnishes us with the notion of continuity.

It would not, then occur to us that time is not a singular, Newtonian construct because our own clocks, the observable quantities "move proportionally to the true time, within an approximation good enough for our purposes. (pg. 3 "Forget Time" Carlo Rovelli). What is difficult to register is the multiplicity of such observable quantities, the billions of clocks that register time in relation to each other and not to a singular, cosmological clock. There is not one "watchmaker" but "billions of them. And these billions operate simultaneously in the split second of the transitional increment of the now.

So, in addition to these billions of simultaneous "clocks" one must also include the simultaneity of memory. As memory is the reduplication of an event, it is also an event in itself and must be included in the all-at-once, even as it is not evidence of fact, but something "lived through".

We live in a non-repeating, non-commutative universe; non-repeating yes, but infinitely copy-able, duplicative. (footnote) But we experience it as repeating and commutative by dint of our position as observer. Given both the variable differences in duration of various levels of stratified partitions of the world/universe, we observe some things as lasting, even enduring longer or expiring faster. And given the susceptibility of our consciousness, the primal levels of association and conjecture, we assume repeatability, the repetition of events going so far as to making an effort to return. And that is fine, sufficient for life, for living. But we are quick to assume a certainty of truth and, what's more, impose this certainty.

(big footnote☺)

 As I must admit, too late in this section to correct, describing this all-at-once with the care and attention it requires, is extremely difficult: new information arrives, some of such validity that it counters, negate what I have set forth, but must be included. Now, I do not assert these things dogmatically, such flexibility for reconsiderations is necessary but not always achievable. Then again, it certainly points to why those who are engaged in the rigidity of dogmatic assertions tend not to read anything outside their realm: contradictions are lethal to dogma.

Reversible? It is speculated as so. (quote) And this could be so, but even in being reversible is it commutative? Reversibility implies commutability, I suppose but reversing, say, event in time does not guarantee the same outcome, the same sum.

EVERETT MANY WORLDS

As footnote

As for this concept of the "all-at-once", it probably could all be explained by referring to, no, deferring to Everett's "universal wave theory", the many-worlds interpretation:

(quote)

My concern here is how this affects our experience of the world.

The watch found in the heath is a watch found in the heath, and the time registered only has immediate relevance as it is related to the time of the things in the heath, at that point.

There is infinity of infinities that are themselves finite.

If we could go back in forth in time is not entering into the same time. It is itself a copy of a copy ever time we enter or re-enter.

Precarious and temporary, transitional.

There then are increments of inifinity but not a spatial-temporally extended infinity.

(NOTE: Eventually, the infinity of the present.)

What is it, then, that we see? How we see? And how we see seeing?

This adds up, as everything, to an immense potential for simultaneity and refraction. Once entering into this space of overlapping incidents, events, ideas, perceptions

This adds up to a world of immense potential for incidents that are multiple and refracted. We live in a simulrefractor

Refractory period,

Our penchant for generalization stemming from our cognitive shortcomings has only agg

What we think as a whole is not really delusion or, not but will suffice as description, an optical illusion, either through refraction or superimposition. Think of things as being layers of transparent and opaque drafts laid out on top of each other. We see a whole from the parts assembled but take a few away and A) the part is survivable as its own and B) the whole we assumed is no longer there.

To see if what there "is" can be separated into the history of itself

We have to invent history

The evidence gathered by and through the defienct organic sensory array should not by any means be the basis for truth.

Are we then deficient? As we are evolved, as consciousness has amplified into

Phenomonon becomes less problematic because we cannot

Composite of subsystems

Emergent
Immersed
Immersiant

Perfects

Flaws